ROUGH PLAN of the WOOD
(Sugg's Orchard & Long Hill Orchard)
Aller, Somerset

Disputed Boundary

Thicket

Horn beam

Ash wood

where the rooks nest

Hermits Apple

Grafted apples

Rounded Slope

plum trees

Uncertain Boundary

Thicketed Slope

ple rafts

chard

Top Orchard

Lombardy Poplars

American Black Walnut

Boundary Walk

old apple trees

Boundary-marking Ash

DEEPER
into
THE WOOD

<small>WRITTEN AND ILLUSTRATED BY</small>

Ruth Pavey

<small>DUCKWORTH</small>

*To All the Plants and
Creatures in the Wood,*

*In the hope they will survive and flourish
and that the Rabbits will return.*

This edition first published in the United Kingdom by Duckworth in 2021

Duckworth, an imprint of Duckworth Books Ltd
1 Golden Court, Richmond, TW9 1EU, United Kingdom
www.duckworthbooks.co.uk
For bulk and special sales please contact info@duckworthbooks.com

© 2021 Ruth Pavey

A catalogue record for this book is available from the British Library.

Typeset by Danny Lyle.

Printed and bound in Great Britain by Clays.

9780715654279

Contents

Introduction

FIRST, A DISCLAIMER . . . THE WOOD I am writing about is small. Lovely as it would be, I cannot invite you to wander deep into glades of beech, under ancient oaks, or to get lost in the gloom of pine forests. Instead I invite you, dear reader, to accompany me as I seek to discover more about the life of this four-acre wood above the Somerset Levels. With its wide views, wild creatures, ash, hazel and apple trees, natural spring, exuberant nettles and thistles, it has much to show, and much to conceal.

The land slopes down below the Aller Escarpment. It was Sleeping Beauty country when I bought it in 1999, with massed brambles throwing a net of thorns over the remaining trees of what I later learnt were Sugg's Orchard and Long Hill Orchard.

The idea had been to buy space to grow trees. But, as my late farming cousin warned, 'anything can happen at an auction' . . . and instead of the intended three open fields, I left the auction room committed to a near-impenetrable piece of woody scrub and derelict orchard. My original idea of planting woodland trees had to expand to include apple tree rescue. Now there is a patchwork of orchard and woodland, but to me it has always remained, simply, 'the wood'.

Taking on a piece of land is like meeting a stranger; there it is with its own character, its own past, its own connections, to be discovered, guessed at. There were no buildings, but a web of plants and creatures fanning out into the surrounding countryside. And maybe, just maybe, people long forgotten have left traces of themselves there, or if not traces, the faintest of vibrations in the air they once breathed.

A Wood of One's Own tells of my first fifteen years of getting to know the wood, but, with a place that grows and changes, there is no coming to the end of the story. Almost the next thing that happened was a sudden, disconcerting surprise . . . the rabbits disappeared.

There used to be plenty of rabbits, living in a warren near the pond. I loved them, protected the young trees against them, took them for granted. As, doubtless, did their predators. It was already worrying that, on my watch, there appeared to be fewer insects, small birds and bats than in 1999. If the rabbits could vanish, as it seemed overnight, a louder alarm bell was ringing.

Across the planet several related reasons, and some that are unclear, contribute to the current, urgent plight of wild flora and fauna. Layered and interwoven, they inform the ways I have been thinking. As well as concerns for wildlife, local history, culture and memory, the lie of the land, the conservation of old varieties of apple, the beauty of the place and the continuing project of planting trees are among the paths I have followed. Some lead into further thicket, so although this book is about going deeper, I should warn you of a certain discursiveness along the way.

Many kind and interesting people have helped me, who, rather than nestling in footnotes, have become part of the story. It moves along with the twentieth-anniversary year of my having become, as I now see it, the present guardian of the wood. Or part-time guardian, as I still live in London.

For the love of them, I have sprinkled in sayings and rhymes to do with the seasons, but also to underline the fragility of some of their age-old assumptions. For example, the expectation that cuckoos will always return to Britain in spring. Where possible I have given attributions, but otherwise the credit must go to Anon.

It has felt strange, writing of 2019 in 2020. But although the beginning of 2020 already feels like the distant past, the coming of the COVID-19 virus has not really been the sudden drop of a guillotine. It may be different in degree, but not in kind, from the disappearance of the rabbits.

The warp of this story is made of the four seasons passing through a Somerset wood. It begins, however, in London, at New Year.

From New Year
to the Vernal Equinox

In not so
wintry winter

Early snowdrops
behind a mossy log

J ANUARY IN INNER LONDON, SOMETIMES SUNNY, often grey, never really cold, provided you had somewhere to live. On New Year's Day, flowers from one season were overlapping with the next. A bumblebee was cruising among them, looking untroubled by the question, is this autumn, or spring?

It *is* troubling, though. Even in the southern parts of Britain we used to be sure of seeing proper frost in winter. However, changes in the climate have been making themselves felt for a long time, as have the effects of modern agriculture. The roses in bloom on New Year's Day were no more remarkable than was the fox I suspected of preparing for her new family under my London garden shed. In short, nature is upset.

But readers will already know that we have much to concern us. I want neither to increase anxiety nor to pretend that all is well. In recording more of what is happening in my Somerset microcosm of the natural world, my hope is only to share a love, and concern, for the wild lives still being lived around us.

While January may no longer be reliably frosty, or April showers bring May flowers, or September offer an Indian summer, at least the encouraging progress from dark winter to light summer does seem still to be in order. In this respect, it is no wonder that seventeenth-century people in Britain were often melancholic. They were living and dying through intermittent years of summers when the sun never shone, of flooded crops, of hunger. As Alexandra Harris tells it in her captivating book, *Weatherland*, they were struggling to survive the Little Ice Age, frequent visits of the wind, El Nino, and the political upheavals that might or might not have been spurred on by them. The wrath of God, it seemed, was abroad.

We hear less, now, of the wrath, more of our own agency. That is, among the people I know and agree with. On the other hand, there are those for whom that seventeenth-century example would only prove that climate change is nothing new, nothing to lose sleep about.

If only that were true . . .

What with one thing and another, it was not till the third week of January that I was packing the car to set off from London, where I mainly live, to Langport, which is near the wood. It had been raining. A neighbour had put hardback books out on her front garden wall for rehoming. Although I understood why she put them there (clearing your parents' house can lead to desperation) I felt sorry to see them getting spoilt in the wet. Especially when many she had put out before had been about natural history. Sure enough, there was Keith Laidler's *Squirrels in Britain*, 1980, its shiny pages beginning to clump together . . . Out of date, but still a gift, because I need to know more about squirrels.

Indoors again I was surprised to read, about the squirrel, 'Probably no animal in the world can match it for its vivacity and sheer cuteness' . . . would a naturalist write like that now? Well . . . 1980 is a while ago, changes in tone can slip in quiet as a cat. Laidler says that squirrels have a special way of dislocating their jaws to allow for two different sorts of gnawing and chewing, that all other mammals have projections in the skull to prevent backward and forward motion of the lower jaw. Spreading the book out to dry, trying a few jaw movements, I was beginning to have doubts about this book.

Most of the journey was wet, with sleet over Salisbury Plain, then towards its end the day brightened into a baby-blue sky with pink mackerel clouds. There was enough light left for a quick look round the wood. From the bottom of the track the orange-stemmed willows stood out good and fiery against the grey-purple of the other trees. The grassy track goes up between an arable field and an orchard with a ditch running down beside the hedge.

In summer the ground is firm enough to drive up, in winter it can be very soggy, or zuggy, as I have learned to call it. In the past, probably the nineteenth century, people took the trouble to dig drains and lay terracotta pipes below the surface. When the drains were new it may have been possible to drive a cart up in any season. Since then the mix of rain and spring water has found ways around the drains.

Walking only takes a few windswept minutes, with the bright willows beckoning. As soon as you are inside the gate it is as though the wind flying across the open land has been put back in its bag, making the wood feel almost warm. Close to and looking up, the colour of the willows gets lost, because the background is now the sky itself, blinkingly bright even in January.

On that afternoon the first thing I noticed would, until a couple of years ago, have been annoying. Now, it was a thrill . . .

under the first old apple tree were scuffling marks, snowdrop bulbs tossed about, and, yes, they definitely were . . . rabbit droppings! The first I had seen for a while.

About rabbits, and their disappearances, although popular history has it that myxomatosis was a man-made disease, it was actually the spreading of a naturally occurring virus that was man-made. To help arable farmers, it was brought from Australia to France, but the then government of the UK decided it was too cruel a disease to import. A Kent farmer imported it anyway, so it is said.

From the 1950s onwards, 80 to 90 per cent of wild rabbits in Britain died. I can attest from my father's reaction that the slow, painful death the disease inflicted was not thought justified by members of the public. Once it was out, there was no stopping it. The only grace was that some rabbits were resistant, and so the population began to rebuild.

Myxomatosis is still here. Because of it, every so often rabbits suffer another wave of illness and death, followed by some restoration of their numbers. Early on in my time of regular travel between London and Somerset, I would pass scores of them on summery evenings, eating the grassy banks of the A303. They stopped doing that a while ago, then in about 2016/17, they vanished from the wood.

Where were they, what had become of them? It was from happening to listen to *Costing the Earth* on Radio 4 in 2018 that I first heard of Rabbit Haemorrhagic Disease. There are two versions, RHD1 or RHD2, both viral, both deadly. They are thought to have been carried here on domestic rabbits imported from China. The difference between the two versions is that with RHD1 the rabbits die on the surface of the ground, with 2 they go down into their burrows to die, so it is flies around the entrance holes that tell the tale.

I am not at the wood every day and could not remember seeing either dead bodies or flies. All I knew was that I liked the rabbits, was grieved to hear of them dying of internal bleeding, missed them, and railed against the international trade in live animals.

However, as every cultivator knows, rabbits are pests because, like us, they delight in eating fresh greens. In winter, the soft bark of young trees will do. As soon as I started planting saplings in 2000, rabbits and deer, undeterred by plastic guards, started eating them. So the saplings needed protective wire enclosures as well. On mass tree-planting sites such as motorway banks you see hundreds of saplings with plastic guards and nothing else to keep them safe. What you do not see is how many gnawing teeth have got in past, under and above the guards. Mass planting assumes this sort of failure, my hand-knitted approach does not.

One spring the rabbits made such progress through the sprouting winter wheat in the field next door that, from the edge of the wood, there was a great ballooning curve of red bare earth expanding into the green. It was clear where the rabbits had started nibbling from, and why spent cartridges show up among the fallen leaves of their, and my, domain. Multiply that amount of damage across fields of young green shoots up and down the country and . . . well, it still does not justify bringing in such a disease as myxomatosis.

According to The Mammal Society website, rabbits count as a naturalised rather than native species, meaning that they were introduced before the twelfth century but were not resident on the land that was to become an island about eight thousand years ago. Current opinion favours the Normans, as opposed to the Romans, for bringing them. They were not, like grey squirrels, introduced for fun. It was because their fur could be worn and their bodies eaten. They flourished, and once they had escaped into the wild, took up a place in the web of life, providing food, clearing ground, entering the imaginative life of children.

Myxomatosis is extremely hard on rabbits, but it may well be that the results of bringing in RHD1 and 2 will be worse, not least because they have 'jumped' species to hares. Rabbits in Britain are now listed as threatened, that is, 'at appreciable risk of extinction'. Hares could follow them.

This risk of extinction depends on how well the rabbits develop resistance, which explains my joy at seeing those droppings in January . . . perhaps this was the beginning of a come-back. With hindsight from the end of the year, I am sad to say that it does not seem to have been a come-back, more a last stand. From that January onwards, my eyes were always peeled for rabbits, whether healthy, sick, dead, or just leaving signs of themselves.

I tried to push the scattered snowdrop bulbs back into the unyielding ground, then set off for the first look round of the new year. The last time I had been there, after Christmas, had been a misty late afternoon. Cobwebs, stretched between dock stalks, were alight with dewdrops. Tight yellow hazel catkins looked ready for spring, but the wood felt shrouded and quiet. On this day, nearly four weeks later, the shrouds were off, a blackbird was singing, tits and robins were about. Here and there, snowdrops were showing.

Heavy clay is not what a snowdrop really wants to grow in, so my dream of a four-acre swathe of white has yet to come true. To give them choice, I planted scattered clumps all over the place, hoping some would spread. It soon appeared that thirsty tree roots helped them to grow, because the bulbs took well to a wooded bank and to being under the old apple tree near the gate (which I call First Tree, not to make this sound like the Garden of Eden but because of its position). So when new trees go in,

Snowdrops by
First Tree
r elders on
the way into
the wood

snowdrop bulbs usually go in around them. Then summer comes and the grass and weeds surge over what is supposed to be a clear space at the sapling's feet.

One of the best things about returning to the wood in January is searching for these snowdrop places, unpicking the grassy thatch of last year and finding, more often than not, green shoots. Some varieties come into flower earlier than others. In the brisk survey I could take before dark, several of the clumps that should have been there were invisible, but quite a few of the milky flowers shone out. Milky is not my description, I am borrowing it from the botanical name, Galanthus, i.e. milk flower. There really is something soft and milky about that shade of white, and the texture of the petals, both more like milk than snow.

I went looking for the best clumps up in the hazel wood where big, many-stemmed stands of hazel have grown out from their former coppicing. Above them runs the boundary separating my land from the steep ash wood above. The big patches of snowdrops were showing through the gloom, but while I was looking for the smaller, newer ones something strange came into view . . . the old wire netting of the mounded boundary had been breached. It looked as though something had pushed it aside, scouring a way down through the fallen leaves, something more like a human than an animal, and possibly equipped with wire cutters.

That bit of the wood is always the first to get dark so I put off trying to investigate closer, holding on to the hope that daylight would make everything look better. There is already difficulty over the boundary further along, I dreaded the thought that it might now be starting above the hazel wood as well.

Somewhere to the west along the hill, owl hoots cheered me up. Even if they were not as close as they used to be, at least they were there, after a seeming absence of more than a year. The rabbits went, then the owls. Rightly or wrongly, I connected these things.

Lead-grey clouds were now hurrying across the sky. Though past 5 p.m., it was still easy to see the way down the open track. Less than a month had passed since that misty afternoon in December, but how different it already felt . . . midwinter chased off-stage, snowdrops advancing. Back at the cottage, the lights were on. Darren, my son, lives there, and had got home early. There is nothing, in my view, more comforting than lighted windows in winter, when you know that it is not some automatic device has switched on the lights, it is someone you want to see.

For the next few days I worked on several things in the wood, mainly to do with the lost line of the boundary between it and the neighbouring woodland. I realise that boundary disputes, while they may be gripping for those concerned, are not so for everyone else. Suffice it to say then, that when, sometime in the early nineteenth century, Sugg's Orchard and Long Hill Orchard were joined into one property, they did not make a neat outline on paper. They lie beside each other on the slope, with Long Hill Orchard jutting up further to the north than Sugg's, then plunging down diagonally to the south-east before meeting the still discernible mounded boundary with Ted's orchard. Ted, the late Ted, was my orchard neighbour. Although it has passed to his son, Philip, I still tend to think of that orchard as Ted's.

The jutting and plunging of the boundary line, long overgrown, then confused by the later cutting of a pathway, is at the root of the territorial trouble. For a long time I tried to ignore it. Then small plastic boxes appeared in the trees, some of them well within my land. They heralded, so I heard, the sort of wildlife survey people are bound to carry out before getting planning permission for development. And, so my cheerful informant added, if the surveyors find dormice or other such creatures, the wishful developer will make sure to kill them before then commissioning another survey to show that the land is empty of protected species.

I dislike conflict, am also a procrastinator, but really, some things you cannot ignore. So along came Patrick the mapper, with a long pole carrying a GPS device and a bag of short stakes, and marked out the boundary as shown on the Land Registry plan. On the ground, it took him an hour or so. When I asked how long it would have taken before GPS was invented, he said about two days, and the result would have been less accurate.

The jutting-up bit went higher than I had expected, and made sense of something my predecessor, Mr Scriven, had told me; that he had allowed a path to be cut through a corner of the land, then regretted it. Wafts of an opening can of worms were unmistakeable, although the neighbouring woodland had by that time changed hands and the threat of development seemed to have receded.

When I got home and told Darren of the mapper's discovery, he was his usual uncompromising self. 'Forget it,' he said, 'you've got enough wilderness already.' In vain did I insist that, though that was so, the boundary needed to be agreed, to prevent further alarms over development. 'You know I'm going to sell it for development anyway,' was his teasing response. At least I hope it was a tease.

The future of the wood does concern me. Establishing an agreed boundary was meant to be a step towards a legal document

to protect it. Alas, that whiff of the can of worms was not misleading and, so far, the day of establishing an agreement is further
away than ever.

∾

The rest of that January visit was taken up with two other
continuing wood projects, the snowdrops and the hope of
perpetuating the old apple trees through grafting. With the
snowdrops it was only a matter of finding and enjoying them,
or occasionally not finding them, in their scattered places.
Under the silvery willow a broken plastic label came to light
saying 'Straf . . .'.

It was just enough for me to recall a snowdrop bought from a
garden near Salisbury, and, in imagination, for the banks of one of
those swift chalk streams to appear, massed with snowdrops on either
side, the clear water racing by over a bed of bottle-green, flowing
weed. Devoted as I am to the River Parrett, which passes through
Langport on its curvaceous way to the Bristol Channel, there is no
denying the extra beauty and emotional pull of chalk streams.

As well as bulb tossing, the scufflers in the wood toss labels
about. 'Straf . . .', or 'Straffan', as I think the snowdrop was
called, was a chunky variety when it went in. If the skimpy ones
near the willow were its survivors, they were not doing very well.
Also near the willow lay a pile of half plum stones, assembled by
a cavity under the willow root. A vole residence, perhaps? There
was no sign of rabbits.

Since my labelling is short-lived, I have long been meaning to
make a plan charting where the different varieties of snowdrop,
and other plants, are growing. People restoring lost gardens often
deplore the lack of old plans . . . an unlikely scenario in this case,
but it would still feel good to have recorded where things are.

In the higher reaches of the wood stand, or lean, two old apple trees. They were the ones that first whispered to me that this land had once been orchards. It was only later, when the solicitor passed on a bundle of old deeds, that I first read the names, Sugg's and Long Hill Orchard. The two apple trees look as though they belong in an Arthur Rackham illustration, so I have always thought of them as Arthur Rackham, or AR1 and 2.

They still sometimes bear fruit, strong, sculptural apples with ribs running down from the blossom end and a red flush where the sun has reached them above the brambles. They are sweet enough to eat, so probably not cider apples. I am not convinced they are both of the same variety. No one, so far, has been able to identify them.

The year before, AR2 had a fair crop. Not only was this a reminder of how good its fruit is, it was also a possible warning. One of its two trunks had recently fallen, so this brave show of fruit could be a swansong. I had certainly taken scions for grafting from it before, but even when voles or rabbits cannot be blamed, labelling is not my strongest suit. To reinforce the chances of perpetuating the tree, I looked for more scions. The fallen trunk was still alive, bringing its higher branches within reach.

Scions are young, straight twigs of the most recent growth, full of bud and vigour. Or they should be. I took two that approximated as nearly as possible to that description, for putting into the soil in a corner of the cottage garden. The idea of this 'heeling in' is to keep them moist but dormant till spring, when they can be invited, with a few deft cuts followed by careful placing and binding together, to become one with a rootstock. The rootstock is chosen to grow the size of tree you want . . . grafting is all about control, having more say about the character of a tree than you would have when planting a pip. The few deft cuts, so I hear, come with practice.

It was with some lopping of brambles and further good intentions that I left the Arthur Rackhams, wishing them a prosperous new season, and more to come. When, in 1999, I had asked the very elderly Mr Scriven about the apple trees I had taken over from him, hoping he would recall some of the varieties or when they had been planted, all he said was that he had given up cultivating them in the 1950s, because the price for apples had fallen so low. It is a fair guess, then, that the surviving trees are at least eighty years old, probably more. To live a hundred years is good going for an apple.

Of the fifteen or so that were still standing in 1999, only about six remain. As with elderly humans, the trick is not to fall, or to be well propped up. However, if they do fall, some apple trees can do what we cannot; put down fresh roots and start again.

The apple coming nearest to perfection . . .

The best-known old apple tree in England is the original Bramley's Seedling. From a pip sown in about 1809 by a girl called Mary Ann Brailsford, it grew into the parent of all the Bramley's Seedling trees ever since. Mary Ann Brailsford's seedling was planted in the garden of her family's cottage in Southwell, Nottinghamshire. Then the family moved and Mr Bramley, a butcher, became its next keeper.

As it turned out to be a vigorous tree with big, tasty fruit, the local nurseryman, Henry Merryweather, asked permission

Hermit's Apple
& its props

to propagate from it. Mr Bramley agreed, if it bore his name. Tempting as it is to see this as a typical case of women, in this case Mary Ann Brailsford, being written out of the story, I suppose Mr Bramley would have said the same, even if the seedling had been planted by Master Brailsford.

Astonishingly, the tree has passed its two-hundredth birthday, but to say that it is still going strong would be misleading. To preserve it as long as possible, Nottingham Trent University has become its guardian and through the help of Julia Davies, staff member and plant scientist, I was able to visit this remarkable survivor. It is a celebrity in Southwell. Rather as Nether Stowey in Somerset has Coleridge Cottage, Coleridge walks, an Ancient Mariner pub, Southwell has Bramley Cottage, The Bramley Apple Inn, a stained glass Bramley window in the Minster.

The old tree was leafless when I saw it, its upper branches bony against the blue sky. The bark was peeling off in some places, moss had settled here and there. There was no mistletoe, just the remains of ivy still attached, and high up, good young shoots. One branch is supported by a robust prop in the shape of a capital I. A Tree Council plaque, suitably green, stands at the foot of the tree, announcing that this is 'one of fifty Great British Trees in recognition of its place in the national heritage', so designated in 2002 to celebrate the Queen's Golden Jubilee.

No one would claim that the tree is flourishing. For it to be alive at all is so remarkable that I asked Julia how we can be sure it really is the original. Through continuous records, she said, plus the fact that the trunks we see now are nearer a hundred than two hundred years old. The original trunk blew down but where it came into contact with the soil it sent out new roots and two new trunks, becoming in effect a second tree.

The continuous record is thanks to the Merryweather family, the nurserymen who first saw commercial potential in the tree. Through assiduous propagation, growing on and marketing ('The finest apple in cultivation is Bramley's Seedling', as their catalogue of 1885 exclaimed) Merryweather's Nursery promoted their star turn.

Julia and I stood looking up at clusters of fresh shoots dotted along the higher branches of the original tree. She says that she and her pupils go easy on the pruning, in order not to stress the tree, and that yes, it does still have new growth but not as much as before. She mentioned Honey fungus, saying that the tree has certainly had it, but that it seems to have departed. She thinks that what is ailing the tree now may be a mixture of old age and the toxic levels of copper and zinc they have found in the soil . . . possibly the residues from well-intentioned efforts at preservation in the past.

Julia and her students are considering a scheme to get those high-up shoots to put down roots, into what sounded like a form of arboreal nappy. The point would be to get rooted offspring, i.e. a clone, without grafting. This led Julia on to say more about cloning, tissue culture, how the university has mapped the tree's genome and is hoping for funding to do more research. This was a moment for me to keep quiet, but there was one question I did want to ask . . . when you take a graft, isn't the resultant tree a clone anyway? It was like those occasions when you speak the only sentence you know in a foreign language, and then regret it.

The answer seemed to be, yes and no. The no, because with grafting there is the possibility of mutations, of 'erosion of the original DNA'. Then, I think in connection with tissue culture, Julia started sketching an imaginary cell on the palm of her hand, with the nucleus here, and around it . . . at this point my notes fade out. I did recognise the word *mitochondrial*, but even fools who rush in have their limits. Also it was cold, Julia had a class to teach, and I wanted to do a quick drawing before going off in search of warmth and coffee.

I then circled the tree again. It is a privilege to look at things in knowledgeable company, but when it comes to taking them in, there is nothing like being on your own with a pencil and drawing book. While the results may be disappointing, just walking around wondering how to fit a big tree on to the page, squinting up, leaning against an old brick wall in the sun, entreating a robin to keep that pose against the moss while you take a picture, then realizing it has already gone, are all ways of getting to see your subject.

Traces are still there of the most dramatic event of the tree's life, when it fell over and then started off again. The original hollow trunk lies along the ground for a few feet before the two newer trunks rear up. With its dark woody knobbles and bright moss, the old trunk looks very much alive. Laid and fixed on to a short part of it is a curious sheet of crumpled bluish metal. It looks as though its placing was meant as a protective gesture, the provision of an awkward sort of dog-raincoat. Julia said that they are unsure why it is there, but are nervous to remove it for fear of damaging the living wood.

In his booklet, *The Bramley*, Roger Merryweather quotes a report from 1943–4, which may explain the raincoat, '. . . action taken to preserve the tree. The recumbent stem is hollow and on its upper surface contains holes. The edges of the holes have been cut back to live bark and the hollow has been filled with molten crude wax from the oil wells of the neighbourhood. The molten wax runs into all crevices before setting like candlewax, and is covered in a skin of bitumen/ asbestos material (black putty) . . .'

So, no nervousness about stressing the tree in those mid-war days . . . decisive action was the thing with, just possibly, the Home Guard at a loose end? Whether the tree has survived because of, or despite this treatment, I leave others to judge. What visiting it proved to me is what a tough plant an apple tree can be. And how, though it may be quixotic to try to keep old ones going, I am not alone.

~

In late winter, Les Davies comes to do the pruning, because I have no aptitude for it. Les leads pruning and orchard management workshops, for which I have seen him advertised as the 'charismatic orchard guru', so how lucky it is that he has not given up on me. Instead he speaks patiently of water shoots and how I must prune them in summer, then hardly raises an eyebrow if there is a great bristle of them waiting for him in winter. This time, he did mildly remark that he might have to visit in summer as well.

We start off in the cottage garden, where he has gradually restored an excellent, unidentifiable old tree. It is a generous cropper, with apples at their best as autumn pushes towards winter. High up where I cannot reach them but the sun can, and so can the jackdaws and blackbirds, these apples turn from yellow-green to great globes of stripy scarlet crimson. Sometimes they get pecked into crescent moon shapes and are still in place in December, when they double as Christmas decorations.

These apples eat, cook and keep so well that my visit to see the original Bramley's Seedling tree gave me ideas . . . maybe this one is a seedling too, and should be propagated and offered to a grateful world. There was, however, a fairer wind behind the Bramley than I could emulate. Mr Merryweather, of its successful launching, describes himself as having been expert in all the skills of training fruit trees by the age of twelve. His father was a head gardener-turned-nurseryman, and they lived in a great age for the breeding of fruit.

So many of our famous apples, pears, plums were bred in the nineteenth century; Cox's Orange Pippin, Egremont Russet, James Grieve, Worcester Pearmain, Conference pear, Comice, Victoria plum. Nurserymen thrived on competing with each other for medals and publicity. At the National British Pear Conference of 1885, for instance, Mr Rivers won First Prize for a new variety. In honour of the occasion, the pear was called 'Conference'.

New varieties of fruit trees are still being bred, often to make them more resistant to disease or to produce sweeter, more marketable fruit. But the buzz of innovation has moved on . . . Silicon Valley, once known as the Valley of Heart's Delight, was then famous for its orchards.

Although it may be too late to make a fortune from the apple I happened to inherit, I did once hit upon a memorable name for it. It was for the Harvest Festival of the London primary school where my job was to work with children, and their parents, whose first languages included Somali, Turkish, Bengali, Arabic. Ignoring the head teacher's scepticism about this irrelevant branch of learning, a group of children and I were working up a presentation. The point, probably new to most people in the hall, was that apples have names.

The fun of useless knowledge did not have many adult champions, but the children took with enthusiasm to pronouncing esoteric names, including Lord Derby, Orleans Reinette, Keswick Codlin. Maybe they sounded no more outlandish to them than words like *library, assembly, capital letter*. To make it easy to say, we called the nameless apple Cottage Best.

All was cheerful as the children held up their apples, taught the audience their names, then quizzed them. Cottage Best was, understandably, the favourite. For some time after that I was often approached in the playground by ebullient children exclaiming, 'Cottage Best'!

∾

After the preliminary in the garden, Les and I proceed to the wood. Over the years he has brought some order to the new apple plantings, although many of them seem to be naturally wayward. This time I took him up to see the two old ones that I call Arthur Rackham 1 and 2, which I had previously not thought worth his attention. I wanted his opinion of their chances of survival. Les is kind and encouraging, so he looked around the dank, brambly space without a hint of scorn, merely saying that they were indeed reaching the end but would benefit from a freer flow of air.

He offered to use the scions I had collected to take some grafts. I have myself learnt how to graft and feel I should not be handing over to an expert. One or two of the grafted trees already growing in the top orchard may well be Arthur Rackhams with lost labels. However, so strong is my wish to be sure of making descendants of those trees before it is too late, I was grateful to pass on the job to Les.

We went up to the higher orchard, he tweaking off various shoots as he went. Over all he was positive, saying the grafts are settling in well, before commenting, 'You're not a fruit-grower, you're doing something different and very good.'

Oh . . . it took a moment to adjust to this, for the 'something different and very good' to outweigh the not being a fruit-grower. When I had had time to reflect that fruit-growers plant trees in straight lines, keep them in order and expect them to

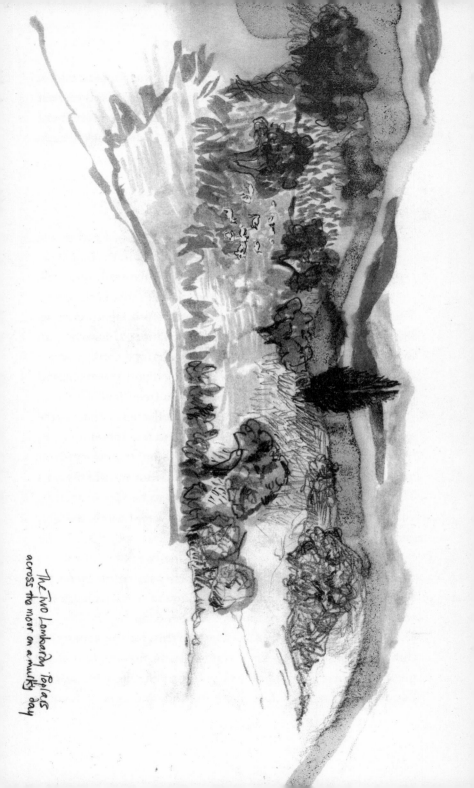

The Two Lombardy Poplars
across the moor on a misty day

produce profitable crops, I had to admit he was right. Besides, he credits me with inspiring him to buy some woodland himself near Cheddar, and that, to me, is a much greater compliment than to be called a fruit-grower.

✦

Invaders and Settlers

✦

There are those who say we should only plant trees native to Britain, that is, species that have grown here since, since when . . . there is more than one time that it could be since; the end of the last Ice Age (c.11,500 years ago) or since Britain was separated from mainland Europe (c.8000 years ago).

There is also imperfect agreement about the tally of native tree species, but let us alight at around sixty. When counting, it seems that it makes quite a difference how many whitebeams (*Sorbus*) you include. Until reading the list of whitebeams in Gabriel Hemery's *The New Sylva*, I had no idea it would be so long, seventeen in all. Starting with English, Common and Arran whitebeam, on it stretches until Bloody and Wilmott's whitebeam, passing Somerset whitebeam on the way.

Native species of tree rank very high with many conservationists because of the natural environment they provide for the wildlife species that have grown up around them. The English Oak, *Quercus robur*, is often cited as the prime example of a tree that supports a host of other creatures; birds, mammals, insects, molluscs, lichens, fungi. At least it does once it is old enough, two hundred years or so. Before that it is only revving up.

To the enraptured tree-planter, the drawback of only sticking to native species is that, although the list of native trees contains many favourites; oak, ash, silver birch, alder, willow, beech, hornbeam, poplar, yew, holly, there are so many more outside the list. Only two of the approximately five hundred worldwide oaks are native to Britain. There are no apples beyond crab apples, just a hedgerow pear called Plymouth pear and our only plum is the sloe. There are no chestnuts, walnuts, sycamores and the only conifer is the pine.

As seemed likely to happen, some eyebrows have been raised at my having chosen to plant non-native species, like cedar, among the ash and field maple already in the wood, so I warm to those opposed to a purist approach. Here, for instance, is Gabriel Hemery, writing of the importance of planting with the threats of climate change and new pests and pathogens in mind. 'Genetic diversity is vital if we are to ensure the "fitness" of trees for an uncertain future . . . Herein lurks the danger of a puritanical approach to "nativeness". It is, at best, an irrelevant obsession, but at worst it can lead to the planting of forests with limited genetic diversity'.

As well as the more recent desire to benefit wildlife and the environment, there are plenty of older reasons underlying tree-planters' choice of species, including novelty and fashion, profit, utility, beauty, food and the delights of learning. Narrative and association are also in the mix. From that list of reasons, my wish to plant two Lombardy poplars would come under beauty and association.

Looking from the fence between my orchard and Philip's across to the moor, I love the sight of two Lombardy poplars standing together like exclamation marks in the flat landscape. With a name like Lombardy they cannot pretend to belong there, but how good they look, their vertical lines bringing excitement to the receding horizontal layers of hedgerow, river embankment, hills.

As soon as I first saw them in the hazy distance, Claude Monet and his love of poplars came to mind. Now that I look through the paintings of poplars reproduced in *Monet's Trees* (Ralph Skea) it is clear that only some of them were of the Lombardy variety. The Lombardy has leaves all the way up its slim form, but Monet represents those that so enthralled him beside the River Epte as having only scraps of foliage on the way up, before bursting out into spreading leafy flourishes at the top.

The book also contains a reproduction of *The Studio Boat*, Monet's painting of his floating studio. It is an enchanting craft, a black wooden rowing boat filled almost entirely by a green cabin with a curved-top roof. It looks enough like a river-borne Rollalong (the Rollalong is my headquarters in the wood, a former builders' site hut-on-wheels) to set off harebrained schemes . . . I have for a while been thinking it a pity to spend all the time earthbound, when there is the River Parrett running so close to the cottage.

I have not located that pair of Lombardy poplars close to, but am told that they are growing beside the river. In the same spirit as I planted cedars as a greeting to those that William Pitt the Elder grew on the opposite escarpment, I want to put in two poplars so they can wave to their fellow non-natives across the moor. Poplars are comparatively short-lived so, to make sure that all four are alive and tall at the same time, this is a project to get on with.

A chat with my conservationist neighbour has made me think that a Black poplar might be co-opted into this scheme. Black poplars are native to Britain but uncommon around Langport, so planting one might count as virtuous, or irrelevantly obsessive, depending on one's standpoint. *The Hillier Manual of Trees &*

Shrubs has our native Black poplar down as 'Manchester poplar, Wilson's variety . . . tolerant of smoke pollution and formerly much planted in the industrial North of England. Native of East and Central England.' Maybe there is a reason for it being uncommon in the South West.

Anyway, in February I called at the wholesale nursery from which many of my young trees have come, in pursuit of two Lombardy poplars. Big ones were available singly. I am not keen on digging the big holes they would need, so we agreed that I could order a bunch of twenty-five saplings, even though twenty-five is a lot when you only want two.

'Well, to be on the safe side, grow on a few more,' advised the nurserywoman, promising to remember that I would have twenty to give away if anyone was interested. I asked to have a look round the stock in the yard. Although this is not a retail nursery, walking round has not been problematic in the past. This time, however, it was, because of stricter rules aimed at keeping out diseases. Shoes should be disinfected, the nurserywoman would have to accompany me, but she was needed in the office. Instead, we talked about plant diseases.

Where Ash Dieback Disease is concerned, disinfected footwear sounds akin to the stable door, only shut long after the horse is out bolting round the countryside. If we had been quicker when this newly discovered fungal disease (*Hymenoscyphus fraxineus*) was identified as the killer of ash trees in Europe in 2006, we could maybe have prevented its importation to Britain. Instead in it came, and was first recorded in 2012 in Buckinghamshire, on young ash from a nursery in the Netherlands. Now it has spread far and wide. It is some years, said the nurserywoman, since they have been allowed to sell or move any ash.

It could be that Ash Dieback Disease would have arrived here anyway, brought in on the wind but, perhaps chastened by the ease with which it did get in, Forestry England and the horticultural trade's attention is now on trying to prevent another unwelcome arrival. *Xylella fastidiosa* is the bacterial disease that began devastating the olive groves of Southern Italy in 2013. Far from confining itself to olives, it can use many plants as a host, including lavender and rosemary. So far (2020) it has not been reported in the UK, so if my not walking round a West Country nursery could help keep it out, it was worth it.

On the way home I was wondering who might like twenty Lombardy poplars. They are often planted to mark boundaries, or along rivers or ditches. The stretch of the River Parrett around Langport is remarkably lacking in trees, which may be deliberate policy, to keep the river unencumbered. The theory that it is good to have rivers encumbered so that the water is slowed down, even to have beavers in to do the encumbering, may not appeal to the engineers dealing with the length of the river most likely to flood.

Just such an engineer, John Rowlands, confirmed that 'Trees are seen as a bit of a risk when it comes to flood defence – most of the banks were constructed centuries ago and they are made up of river silts. The stability of these embankments relies on a good grass sward with a fibrous root system but trees undermine the structure by putting out big roots which are often a way for water to seep along. These may become voids that cause the tree to rock and eventually fall, taking most of the bank with it. Nobody wants a flood bank with a hole in it . . .'

Well no, put like that, the wonder is that any trees are allowed along our stretch of the river at all. John went on to say, 'trees in the right place are part of the solution – the benefits come from planting upland, which slows the flow . . . but having beavers on the Levels may not be the most admired method of flood management'. I love the way he words that, so tactful, so suggestive of all those who might not admire the beavers and their works. Beavers are already doing well in Devon, maybe they will arrive of their own accord, as did the back-from-the-brink-of-extinction otters.

One thoughtful landowner to whom I offered the poplars baulked at the name Lombardy, then the nursery reported that, to their surprise, they had run out of Lombardy saplings for this season. So that was something to worry about later, although not the end of my feeling either furtive/justified about planting non-native species.

There was a sapling crying out to be moved from the cottage garden. It would have preferred to be sown directly into a permanent place at the wood, except that tree seedlings there only grow an inch or two before getting munched off. It was a walnut, and not a common walnut, either. Its parent is majestic and enormous and, just like the Lombardy poplar, its name is uncompromising as to its origin: American Black Walnut.

The responsibility for this transatlantic settler racing upwards in a Somerset garden lies only with me, but it is the indirect consequence of Alexandra Harris giving a talk about her book, *Weatherland*, at the Wells Literary Festival. It was a moody November evening, just right for a thought-provoking work about the weather, and dark by the time we came out. Stewards were there to shepherd us, and so were barriers to discourage any straying from the path.

Then came a reason to stray. On the way back through the first courtyard of the Bishop's Palace, a huge, handsome tree appeared, in all the splendour of its autumn leaves. It had, unsurprisingly, been there when we went in, and for nearly two centuries before that, but what made it now so compelling was the floodlight dramatizing its ochre yellow in the night. Hoping there might be a label attached to its trunk, I stepped over the barrier. Instantly, a steward appeared, but when he was showered with excited questions he tossed health and safety aside, joining me on the wrong side of the barrier and relating what he knew of the tree.

It was an American Black Walnut, and if we looked round the other side he would show me where it was once struck by lightning. The floodlighting could only do so much against the November dark, so the scar was easier to imagine than see. After this lightning strike, fears for the tree's survival had prompted the planting of a replacement. The big tree lived on, however, and now the younger one is getting big too. As we regained the path I picked up a fallen nut, thanked him, and left.

Whoever he was, I thank him again for letting me take the nut. It germinated readily in a pot, then moved all right into the cottage garden, and was now showing a no-nonsense approach to getting on with its life's work of growing into a tall tree, potentially a hundred and sixty feet tall, as I read with some misgiving.

On a bright February day, I set about digging it up from the garden where it had been for two years. Some trees are more tolerant than others about being moved. It depends how their roots form and how easy it is for the transplanter to take them with soil attached. Walnuts dislike being disturbed, having a tap root that quickly goes down deep, with a spidery set of side roots that make nothing like a desirable root ball.

Knowing this from previous encounters, I traced the errant side roots carefully, as they set off for places they should not have been, like under the rhubarb patch. I left digging down beside the tap root till last, but then was shocked . . . care notwithstanding, it was torn right across. Poor tree . . . The only consolation was to think how a hundred and sixty feet might have been excessive, that a torn tap root would surely result in a more modest tree.

As a matter of regrettable fact, the growth of the common walnuts I have already planted in the wood is much inhibited, not so much by their transplantation as by the squirrels' taste for stripping their bark. At least I had assumed it was the taste they like, but Keith Laidler says that bark stripping and scent-marking is also part of their system of communication, both for territorial and breeding purposes. Having used the decorous term 'scent-mark', Laidler then conjures a less decorous image by explaining, 'To scent-mark correctly, . . . the grey squirrel has to project a jet of urine at right-angles to its body'. Anyone familiar with tomcats will know that this is a not a unique accomplishment.

Squirrels are not fussy about which trees to use. Horse chestnuts have also suffered in the wood, and now hornbeam. It depends how old the trees are. Very young they are too bendy, over about twenty their bark is getting too tough. We are all meant to be culling grey squirrels, but setting lethal traps or shooting are beyond me. So, come friendly raptors, and drop on Aller . . . Pine martens would be welcome too.

Grey squirrels count as an *invasive alien species*, making it sound as though they came here on purpose, with aggressive intent. Which may be an accurate description of the Vikings, but not of grey squirrels. They made the long sea journey, presumably in cages, from America, brought in as a new delight in the nineteenth century.

It took some tenacity to get them established, a process in which the zoologically minded ninth and tenth Dukes of Bedford were active. The fact that it gradually became a successful introduction, that has since proved to be a huge blunder, does not justify vilifying the creatures themselves. All they did was survive, adapt and breed.

I planted the American Black Walnut (calling it an *incomer* might be more neutral than *alien*) on a February day when the snowdrops had almost finished and pale yellow narcissi, nearly native, were coming into flower. It stands in a gap overlooking

Philip's orchard, so will get enough light. Although I know that other plants are not supposed to grow under walnuts, grass, elder, brambles, dock, periwinkle and lily of the valley are all able to, at least under young ones, so it seemed worth slipping in some snowdrop bulbs. If the tree is so lucky as to get big it will shade out those others, or dispatch them with chemical emissions from its roots. By that time, I will not be there to worry about it.

∾

Further to the rights and wrongs of native and non-native planting, the Royal Horticultural Society (RHS) has been carrying out interesting research at its garden, Wisley. The *Plants for Bugs* project is posited on the recognition that biodiversity is under global threat, that insects are essential members of that diversity, therefore gardeners should be careful about growing the plants that suit insects best. The project divided plants into natives, near-natives or exotics. By near-native they mean plants from the northern hemisphere, exotic, those from the southern.

Starting in 2010, the first four years were spent gardening, trapping, hoovering, observing, above all, counting. It took the next six to process all the results. The set-up was strictly methodical, with thirty-six 3 x 3 metre beds in two different parts of the garden, each bed planted with native species, near-natives or exotics. The invertebrates were classified as pollinators, such as bees, plant dwellers such as ladybirds, and ground dwellers such as woodlice. The details are on the RHS website, including pictures of the hoover, a 'Vortis suction sampler', which looks heavy and to require the use of ear muffs. The report does not mention if the suctioned invertebrates survived the experience.

From a non-purist point of view, the results were quite encouraging . . . 'Any planting is better than none, and garden plants from all regions in our experiment supported a good number of invertebrates', also, the denser the planting, the better. The research confirmed that native plants are indeed the best, but only marginally so . . . the near-natives attracted less than 10 per cent fewer invertebrates, the exotics, about 20 per cent fewer. For pollinators the exotics, like the African daisy, were good at extending the nectar-collecting season.

The recommendation is, 'To support invertebrate abundance in gardens and other cultivated green spaces, choose plantings biased towards UK native and near-native plants and encourage dense vegetation . . . exotic plants should not be dismissed, however . . .' How evocative is that word 'abundance', at least when applied to the creatures we favour, like butterflies, moths, bees, now so much less abundant than they were only a decade or so ago. Recent books about nature rarely omit to mention the phenomenon known as *shifting baselines*, of which more later.

Meanwhile, I had noticed that phrase 'other cultivated green spaces' in the recommendation quoted above, and asked one of the RHS scientists if it was fair to extrapolate from the findings of a garden-based experiment to include orchards and trees. Here is part of her reply, 'Managing woodland does stretch the definition of a garden space a little, though orchards are classically managed areas with cultivated fruiting trees, even if some are simply selections of natives such as hazel. In a woodland setting that isn't highly sensitive habitat (e.g. ancient woodland) and which is being 'gardened' to some degree then I feel there is indeed some benefit, particularly for pollinating insects, to using non-natives in the mix'.

Hurrah . . . so I am not doing anything too bad. The wood cannot pretend to be ancient, given that most of it was known within living memory to have been orchard. Spurge laurel does occur there, however. This is one of the plants indicating that a wood is ancient, i.e. has been there for more than four hundred years, and the huge hazels, long bursting out from their former coppicing, are clearly old.

Struck by a statistic given in the RHS research, that the average garden is planted with only 30 per cent of native species, I have done a rough audit of the trees in the wood. In the scrub woodland of 1999, almost everything was native except for apples and plums. There were about ten main species; oak, willow, field maple, elm, dogwood, ash, hawthorn, blackthorn, hazel and elder. To these I have added whitebeam, birch, box, holly, hornbeam, mountain ash and crab apple. With near-natives, the count rises by another twenty or so, with one solitary exotic, a drimys, which was given as a present and has always looked as though pining for its native South America. That works out at about half native, half near-native.

While these sums concerned trees, doing them also made me wonder why I have not planted more native flowers as time has gone by. In part, it was the way many of those I did plant got eaten, but it was also that flowers like poppies and cornflower declined to flourish, so it was discouraging. Now the rabbits are so few it would be good to try again, with better attention to 'right plant, right place'. In pursuit of this idea, I commissioned a survey by Emorsgate Seeds.

Donald MacIntyre and colleagues started this company in 1980, to supply wildflower and grass seed to those wishing to plant 'weeds', as other incredulous seeds merchants saw it. One of these weed sowers must be the Prince of Wales, because his feathery crest appears on the catalogue. Donald MacIntyre's daughter, Laurie, came to visit the wood and was touchingly positive, describing it as 'a mosaic of habitats including pond, wet ditches, dense scrub, woodland, orchard and grassland which provides a refuge for wildlife'.

Laurie was diplomatic about the management that has resulted in the fenced sward becoming 'quite rank', recommending that it could either be cut before the sheep go in, or allowed to become tussock grassland, which requires 'minimal maintenance'. Maybe to console me for the latter suggestion, with its seeming acceptance of defeat, she emphasised the value of tussock grassland to wildlife. Here and there among the tussocks she recommended clearing patches for field scabious, common knapweed, wild carrot and other such appealing plants.

There are areas beyond the sheep enclosure where I will probably take her advice, but the fact is, I have long resented the arrival of the tussocky grasses and of sedge for the way they sit themselves down on top of the finer grasses and smaller plants, seeming to crow over their capacity to dominate. If I really believed that letting them do so might lure in such vanishing beauties as snipe, maybe it would be different. As it is, I still harbour dreams of control, not only for the grasses but around the pond and marsh as well, where the willows are getting too big, casting too much shade. Doing this project so long does bring home how things are always changing . . .

Things are always changing, and being forgotten. As soon as I read the name Sugg's Orchard on the deeds Mr Scriven handed down, I wanted to know who Sugg was, and when he had lived and given his name to the land that was now mine. But Ted, my late orchard neighbour, had been dismissive of this idea, saying that *zug* was just another word for soggy mud, not a name. For a long time I contented myself with imagining Sugg, placing him in the ninth century, with a walk-on part in the story of King Alfred the Great's surprising appearance in Aller. (Aller is the parish

to which the wood belongs.) But I have not forgotten him, and
have since been developing another Sugg story, this time based
on written evidence.

The new Sugg is living in the eighteenth century, and has
arisen with the help of the historian who probably knows more
about Somerset's recorded past than anyone else. I first came
across Robert Dunning's name twenty years ago, when beginning
to look along the local history shelf of Langport Library. He had
been engaged in writing the Somerset volume of the *Victoria
County History*. When I asked the librarians about him, and even
the publishers of a 1970s book of his, the answers were so vague
that it seemed that he, too, might be part of the past. Much
more recently he was listed on a programme at Brendon Books
in Taunton. 'Of course he's alive!' was the reply to my query, and
yes, they would put me in touch with him.

And so it came about that Dr Dunning was waiting for me
on the corner of Taunton Bus Station. We walked by watery ways
to his house, where I was introduced to his wife, who was very
welcoming, and their half-Bengal cat, rather more reserved. I had
brought Mr Scriven's bundle of old deeds related to the ownership
of the wood, but first we went through a list of questions, about
field names, land use and ownership, tracks, hedgerows, parish
boundaries, enclosures, monasteries, drainage, King Alfred,
Italian prisoners of war.

If my notes of that morning do not reveal precise answers, they
do convey Robert's willingness to set off in all sorts of directions,
with a book title here, a geologist there, a suggestion for getting in
touch with the descendants of Italian prisoners of war through a
local double-glazing business. 'Time out of mind' I have written
down next to a question about when mounded banks started to
be used to mark boundaries. As to when land on the slope of
Aller Hill might have come into cultivation, Robert risked being

more specific, pinpointing around 1300 as probable, when an increase in population drove people to use more marginal land.

Pleasing though it would be to picture apples growing on that slope since 1300, it might be more realistic to imagine strips of beans, rows of wispy wheat or oats, root crops like parsnips or skirret not doing very well on the heavy clay, sheep at pasture, pigs rootling under trees. Being marginal, the land may have kept coming into and going out of cultivation, and not settled down to bearing apples till the eighteenth century.

About tracks, I was interested in a rumour that the one from the road to the wood had been part of a longer one, right from Bowdens, the area at the top of the escarpment, past the wood, across the road and on to the River Parrett. It was in my mind that if there had been an old way down there, it could reinforce my hope that the outgrown hedgerow, with its mixture of more than six woody species, might count as 'ancient'.

At the mention of tracks Robert fetched a copy of *The Old Straight Track* by Alfred Watkins, saying in a non-committal way that it was worth a look. First published in 1925 and setting out Watkins's theory of ley lines, this edition had been produced in Glastonbury with a cover embellished with mystic curlicues. When I later borrowed a copy from the library it came in a more recent edition, without mystic curlicues but with an introduction by Robert Macfarlane.

If I had no expectation that *The Old Straight Track* would answer my question about a route down from Bowdens, there is something very intriguing about a theory that, though dismissed by some as nonsense from the moment Watkins presented it to the world, has gone on to persuade untold thousands of people of its worth, and to sprout a spiritual dimension he never intended. Glastonbury, a cradle of much of this, is so nearby that I felt I must give Alfred Watkins the time of day.

Sugg, of Sugg's Orchard, Robert said would certainly have been a person, but that that did not mean Ted was wrong about *zug*, that there are plenty of people called Marsh. A much less earthy-sounding name then arose, that of the author of *The Concise Oxford Dictionary of English Place-names* . . . Eilert Ekwall. Being impressionable when it comes to scholarship, I was later excited to read of a professor at home in Swedish, English, German, Latin, with Celtic and Scandinavian philology at his fingertips. He spent most of the first half of the twentieth century at Lund University pursuing, among other things, the derivations of English place-names.

As a sidestep towards my quarry, I looked up place-names in Ekwall's dictionary starting with Sug . . . Sugnall, Sugwas, Sugworth. Being unsure of how accurate a passage I had navigated through the abbreviations, to arrive at 'sug' meaning 'bird' in Old English, I consulted with my brother. Yes, he replied, *sugga*, or *sucga*, does mean bird in Old English, and, for refinement, a *haysugge* is a hedge sparrow. How pleasing it was, to find that the name of the orchard might refer to birds rather than soggy mud.

When we started looking at some of the deeds, Robert extracted a reference to Sugg's Acre as being part of Aller Field. So Sugg had not only an orchard named for him, he had an acre as well. In a follow-up email, Robert said that this naming could be to do with the parcelling out of land at the time of the Enclosure Act of 1797, and would I like his help in looking it up in the records at the Somerset Heritage Centre . . . ? Yes, please.

Somerset opened its ('state of the art') Heritage Centre on a distant, hard-to-find development site in 2010. No bus takes you there, but once you do manage to find it, there is the sense of being welcomed to a desert island, with advice about not missing the sandwich and coffee van at lunchtime. I picture this van and its driver bringing cheer to isolated places of work, scattered across the many acres of agricultural land disappearing under new developments.

I had been to the Heritage Centre once, quite a while ago. Since then the roads seemed to have changed so I was late for my meeting with Robert, but found him at a table, noting down names from a thick book. The names were of fifteenth-century clergy of the diocese of Bath and Wells, he said, pointing out the freshness and clarity of the writing on the bound vellum pages. There was a mark rather like a watermark on one page, as though a seed-head had become embedded in the vellum . . . maybe where the animal whose skin had become the vellum had had a scar, Robert thought. Immediately, an image of a long-dead beast sprang to mind, its shoulder bloodied as it laboured to pull the plough. In the modern, sleek surroundings of the centre, this ghostly touch of real, raw past life felt oddly shocking.

We collected a map from the desk, 'A Plan of the open and commonable, ARABLE LANDS in the Parish of ALLER in the County of Somerset'. It is a handsome document on parchment with fine black writing, the dividing lines between the plots picked out in golden yellow. The surnames written inside the divisions relate to the allocation of land for the 1797 act of enclosure, or inclosure, as it spells it.

It took a while to recognise anything. What is called South Field turned out to be the fields east of Aller, which became clear once I had seen a junction where the track down from the wood crosses the road and goes on towards the moor. The very track that I want to know more about, although incomplete on this plan. Towards the moor it is called Lower Road. The part I use starts off Wallis's Road but only reaches as far as the current sheds and Philip's new bungalow, where Wallis seems to have been allocated a skinny, backwards-L-shaped parcel. Then it becomes

Farrows Road; no mention of Sugg, maybe Farrow was working Sugg's Orchard by then.

My land was not part of this 1797 share-out. Only its lower boundary appears, with the words 'Ancient Inclosed Lands' and no names attached. I had been under the impression that the enclosure of all common land had been exploitative, causing the peasant cultivators to lose their rights to shared fields, pasture, firewood, but Robert said that on this occasion it would have been a move to improve upon the old strip system, making agriculture more efficient. Commissioners would have been in charge, with the allocation of land carried out fairly, by agreement.

The idea of the bearers of those names on the plan, the Wallises and Hawkers and Kiddles and Sawtells, the Richardses and Farrows and Peddles and Hydes, all agreeing that they had been fairly treated does sound optimistic. Argument and grumbling, followed by resignation seem more likely, as they got used to doing things a new way. Or maybe had to leave rural life altogether, in search of work in the developing factories and mills.

The trouble, says my sister-in-law Louise, with pursuing this sort of local history is that you soon disappear down a rabbit hole. How easy it is to see what she means . . . all I wanted was to know who Sugg was. But now a reason had popped up for asking, who were Wallis and Farrow?

Robert set me in front of a microfiche viewer, looking at little patches of fuzzy writing, grey on grey. The idea was to check if Sugg was there, among late eighteenth-century records of field ownership in Aller. As far as I could see, he was not. Then we looked at the 1838 tithe map. The property of the Wallises, of the L-shaped scrap of land and Wallis's Road, seemed to have expanded. Robert Wallis is the owner/occupier of Long Hill Orchard (now mine) Vincent and Samuel Wallis owned Misbrook Orchard (now Philip's, formerly Ted's). Misbrook is not a name

Doreen, Ted's widow, recognises. The risks of falling down Louise's rabbit hole were becoming all too clear. So away with you, Farrow and Wallis, Sugg is my only bird . . .

Before we parted, Robert lent me a novel by Peter Benson, *The Levels*. When I arrived home it was a tonic to turn to it, joining the landscape and company of people living near Langport, at Muchelney, c.1960. A time, as the novel tells, when a local boy could still learn from his father how to weave eel traps, while imagination took him far beyond such a traditional way of life. It is not that, even sixty years later, Somerset has lost all its willow weavers (although it is losing its eels) but the chances of learning the skills of willow weaving within your own family have surely got slimmer.

One for the mouse,
One for the crow,
One to rot,
One to grow

That rhyme about seed sowing speaks of a more tolerant attitude towards our fellow species than industrial agriculture has any room for. Now that the loss of the wildlife that was all around us has become so urgent, I wish I had had surveys of birds, insects and wild plants done when I first took on the wood twenty years ago. It would have given something against which to measure what has happened since.

But the truth is, I never thought of it. It was a balancing act to be working in London and planting trees in Somerset at the same time, so I just made diary notes of what I saw, or thought I had seen. Nor did it occur to me that many of the creatures range further afield, meaning that though the four acres of the wood remained a chemical-free, fairly wild place for them, that might not be the same nearby.

During this year of exploration I was determined to have some surveys done. Despite having reservations about how much good it does those individual creatures, that we are counting them, I did want more expert human eyes and ears on the case. Having already published a book about the wood was a help, because people interested in the natural world, some qualified to carry out surveys, began to get in touch.

One such was Roger Dickey, who organises local talks for Somerset Wildlife Trust. We soon struck a deal, that I would give a talk and he would come to the wood to survey the birds. The talk was to be later in the year, the survey in spring, with a prior look-around in February.

Roger was in the Army. He had been a gunner, and has to keep his hearing aids tuned specially high to hear birds. This endeared him to me, although I felt that his former profession might be glinting through when he said he was having difficulty making sense of the place. The Army does, after all, value order. More disconcerting was his observation that the crows are really rooks . . . after all those years of me thinking that they were crows. Not only thinking, but writing about and drawing them as crows . . . this revelation took some getting used to.

A thrush started singing as we walked round, which prompted me to speak wistfully of nightingales. I told how a friend had claimed to hear them close by, but that I had only hoped it was nightingales I once heard from a thicket of brambles, when it was more likely to have been robins.

Some of the stands of bramble, tall as cottages, have skirts of new growth sweeping down. Hidden underneath are elder trees, struggling to uphold this cascade. Approving of the cover, Roger said it was just the sort of habitat nightingales would like, but that did not mean there would be any. Even at Swell Wood on the opposite escarpment, where they used to be every spring, they have not been heard for a while.

To enable research into their distribution and movements, Roger rings birds. He asked if he could put up nets to catch them in the wood, assuring me that they were not harmed in the process. Then he let slip that the birds struggle in the pockets of the net before being ringed and released. In an instant I was back in the 1960s, in a fruit cage, detailed by an elderly relative to pick raspberries. The netting of the cage was a grid of grey string. The torn and desiccated corpses of small birds were tangled up in it, while some were not yet dry and might even be still alive. Two birds were flying about inside, which it was possible, although not easy, to guide out through the open gate.

Being brought up not to make a fuss, I then picked raspberries and shut the cage door after me, little suspecting that this image of prolonged, doomed struggle would be imprinted for life. It has prevented me from ever making a thorough job of netting soft fruit, or brassicas, or any other plant that both we and the birds like. An un-thorough job, a sort of deterrent hairnet on sticks, often seems to work well enough.

He was not to know any of this, but Roger could see that the netting idea was unwelcome, so did not persist. At which I felt bad about hindering science and conservation. Ringing birds gives data, he says, and without data we can't do anything. Which all makes sense, except, maybe, the imperative to Do Something . . .

Nightingales have come back to Knepp, the Sussex estate of Isabella Tree and Charlie Burrell, because they stopped so much Doing (in their case, farming) and let nature take over.

The non-human inhabitants of this planet were perfectly able to get on with their lives before we humans knew so much about them, from our hunting, farming, domesticating, naming, breeding, watching, counting, drawing, filming, not to mention writing. One telling point Isabella Tree makes in her book, *Wilding*, is that we should step back, intervene less. She says that though conservationists are sometimes successful in nurturing particular declining species by working to give them a more suitable environment, it is the ecosystem as a whole that needs the chance to recover, free from human activity. The Knepp project and her book are inspirational. Pigs may, however, fly sooner than human beings stop intervening.

After Roger had departed I went to meet Tony Anderson, to discuss contributing to 'Ebenezer Presents', a programme of events held in Aller in circumstances of the most pleasing eccentricity. The programme is a mixture of talks, films and performances. It was started by Ian Constantinides, who had converted the Ebenezer Baptist Chapel in Burrowbridge into a dwelling. I have not heard what any of the remaining Baptist congregation felt about the cosmopolitan events now filling their old chapel; perhaps some were glad it was still a place of meeting. Then, all too young, Constantinides died and the chapel had to be sold.

The homeless 'Ebenezer Presents' might have folded, but Sarah Constantinides, Tony Anderson and one other 'Ebenezer' wanted to keep it going. They were offered part of the Seed Factory in Aller. As with the chapel, this is a building with a past, housing first a milk factory then a business pioneering the embedding of seeds into biodegradable tapes, to make them easier to sow.

Needing bigger premises, Seed Developments moved on, and 'Ebenezer Presents' was able to occupy the lofty upstairs rooms.

Tony invited me to have a look, to get an idea of what giving a talk there would be like. He ushered me into a friendly, bohemian space with unmatched chairs looking as though they too had enjoyed rich and varied previous lives. My immediate impression was that it would be very cheerful with a lot of people inside. If ill-attended, it could be rather too like that haunting scene in Ingmar Bergman's *Fanny and Alexander*, in which the children wander alone among eerie puppets. Still, the stage looked almost cosy, with a grand piano and several dogs, most of them toys but one, possibly, a real dog stuffed.

My only previous encounter with these events had taken place when roadworks in Aller had blocked its only through street. It was getting dark, a rainstorm was in full swing and an extraordinary number of vehicles were parked along the road, with people bent forward, trudging against the wind to get into the village. All unknowing, I got caught up in this seeming disaster and asked what was happening. 'Kate Adie's here!' was the reply which, given her association with war zones, was striking. Apparently she was due to give a talk at the Seed Factory, meanwhile the roadblock was foxing everyone.

This experience had suggested that 'Ebenezer' talks were starry affairs, to which people were prepared to travel on stormy nights, and made me feel hesitant. But Tony was very positive, saying that the wood was so local he was sure of a good audience. Also, his plan was that this event should be in June, so that afterwards anyone who liked could come on a woodland visit. It was to check the logistical implications of this idea that we had met with enough time to see the wood in the light.

As I already knew from previous celebrations, getting a crowd of people up there has its problems. The track takes off at an abrupt right angle from the road, without concern for visibility. Or it did then, Philip's building project has entailed safety improvements, with the cutting of a 'splay'. There is still little space to park and, once in the wood, plenty of opportunities to trip up. The rabbits may have vanished but their holes remain.

Given my wish for the rabbits to return, it is hard to know which would be better, laboriously to fill in their old holes, so that any survivors would be burrowing afresh. Or to conserve their previous works, making it easier for them to re-occupy, at the risk of the holes still being infected. In such speculations do I sometimes beguile a sleepless hour, when it might be better to be up and emailing experts at the 'University of Rabbits', as, according to Radio 4, the University of East Anglia is sometimes known.

Once Tony and I had taken a turn around the wood and the pinkish light was fading over the Quantocks, we went to a pub in Huish Episcopi, a village adjoining Langport. The pub is known for its live music and links to the folk singers who sang to Cecil Sharp in the early 1900s. When I first visited it there was still no bar, just a stone-flagged room with kegs in one corner. However, despite liking its old-worldiness and the swallows swooping in and out of their nests in the thatch over the door, I did not find it the most welcoming place for a Londoner, so have not been there much. Tony, after forty years living in nearby Burrowbridge, feels more at ease there, although still did not claim to be an insider.

Tony is a writer, an authority on the Caucasus, and it emerged that his wife, Lucy Willis, is a painter who had been to the Ruskin School of Art some years after I had been a student there. So we were soon launched into news of a former Ruskin tutor living locally, and plans for turning the proposed 'Ebenezer' event and woodland walk into some form of get-together. June was still far off, making it easy to enjoy talking about.

In like a lion, out like a lamb

There was more of the lion than the lamb in March. The Vernal Equinox is meant to be windy, but the gales, and warnings of gales, did not restrict themselves to the days around 20 March. Ever since the notorious failure to warn of the Great Storm in 1987, weather forecasters tend to be cautious, but I did take them at their word about wild winds on my first March journey to Somerset and avoided the higher ground of Salisbury Plain.

There are lower, slower but more sheltered ways. One leads past a lake, with spreading cedars in parkland on the other side. When I went that way in February the cedars were wreathed in white mist, even the sheep looked mysterious. This time the cedar branches were full of movement and the busy, ruffled lake was alive with gulls, swans, ducks. Centuries have passed since the lake was dug and the cedars were planted, long enough to give them the air of always having been there. But, as with so much parkland across Britain, the tranquillity of that landscape belies its origins. Sugar money paid for it, a fact that deserves acknowledgement, even if there is no changing the past.

This being March, even after a slow journey, it was still light when I arrived in Langport. An outburst of late afternoon sun made everything look welcoming. Darren had just got back and said, to my pleased surprise, that the wood had been looking very nice as he drove past. Such praise does not often escape him so, on the way there, I wondered if the plum blossom was out already. No, there was only a hint of white, nothing to catch the eye. Instead, the sun was full on the red/orange willows, making them leap forward from their sombre neighbours, demanding to be seen.

The first good thing to notice was that Steve had been in and cleared behind the electric fence. When the idea of borrowing sheep as mowers became a reality, the hope was that they would provide a greener, easier way to keep the patches of orchard open than petrol-powered mowing. In went the electric fence, with a margin between it and the thicket.

For the first few years I strove to keep the margins clear. The sheep were playing their part, but there was a Painting-the-Forth-Bridge element to trying to stop the electric fence from disappearing under the greenery, and so failing to conduct electricity. I came to dread it, and was happy when Steve Joyce, gardener, took on the task, which he does much better and faster. My methods did not involve petrol, his do. There it is, sometimes you have to compromise.

I love to arrive and find the sheep ensconced. They settle in quickly and get on with being sheep, drumming their pathways between their preferred spot up in Long Hill Orchard and lower down by the gate, where Laura, their keeper, puts out water and molasses-with-salt lick for them. To my eye, they enliven the scene.

For a variety of reasons, some environmentalists may disapprove of my taking pleasure in sheep. One objection is that to keep grass down, as opposed to letting it grow long, is to deprive small vertebrates and invertebrates of a place to live. Sheep also get a very bad press for doing what I want them to do, especially on hills and mountainsides, where their constant nibbling prevents the regeneration of trees.

Then there is the question of beauty, an irritant to some concerned with the future of the natural world. To see sheep as decorative additions to the landscape is to look through the old-fashioned viewfinder of pastoral writing and painting. It is to place humanity outside and above everything else living on the planet, instead of admitting that we are just a part of the whole system . . . an overweening part, but no more than that, and dependent upon it.

In answer to my imaginary critics . . . first those who would let the grass grow (which a lot of it does anyway, outside the sheep enclosure). If I had not taken on land that had been allowed to go wild, I think I would have higher hopes of 'rewilding'. But non-intervention had allowed so triumphant a spread of brambles across the orchards that it could almost have been called a monoculture. I am not complaining that a small piece of neglected ground should not turn out as marvellously diverse as has the 3,500 acre Knepp Estate, helped along by old breeds of cattle, pigs, ponies and deer.

However, I think a few of those Knepp miracles could have happened; with two oak trees in the hazel wood as a source of acorns, jays to distribute them, patches of blackthorn for cover, the recipe for young oaks surviving the hungry deer was in place . . . but none were to be found. As already regretted, no nightingales have taken advantage of the bushy cover on offer to them, let alone turtle doves. When coarse weeds started to spread in the reclaimed orchard grass I once saw a flock of goldfinch in the thistledown. Only once, and I still await the effusion of Painted Lady butterflies that so helpfully arrived to deal with the thistles at Knepp.

As to finding nature beautiful, in however backward-looking, Wordsworthian a way, I was brought up to it. My father, and the aunt who cared for me after my mother died, were both

born in the nineteenth century, when Wordsworth had been
dead for less than fifty years. There is no undoing the way you
were introduced to the world. Recently on the radio I heard a
young-sounding publisher speaking of nature-writing, stressing
the importance of getting away from the old model of following
the seasons, observing the weather, extolling the beauties . . . oh
dear, here I am, following the year, snowdrops, skyscapes and all.
If that needs an excuse, it is that the leopard cannot (and does
not really want to) change its spots.

Snowdrops were finished when I took that first March
look-around but the daffodils were out, fluttering and dancing,
except for the fallen ones shredded by pretty yellow and black
snails. Violets, white, mauve, deep purple, were dotted along
the boundary walk. They always grow there, moving about from
one stretch to another. I used to worry if they did not reappear
where they had been the year before, but am now accustomed to
their ways. Much to my excitement, a rabbit was hurrying across
Philip's orchard.

Less pleasingly, something (deer?) had bitten off the snakes
head fritillary flowers. Pear blossom was coming, the pond was
quite full, there were plenty of rooks and some birdsong, mainly
from tits and blackbirds. I listened in vain for the thrush Roger
the ornithologist had identified. The sky was pearly, then yellow-
grey, with dark tatters of cloud once the sun had gone down.

Someone had rough-cut the hedge beside the track. This
cutting with a flail does not make such a good thick hedge for
birds, moths, butterflies and other creatures to live in as does
traditional hedge-laying, but is a much quicker method. It also
gets done without my even knowing who does it, so I am grateful
for that. Admittedly, a well-laid hedge would be better, but the
gashes left by the flail do green up soon enough, and the wrens
still seem able to find cover there.

The hedge is mainly of what I would call thorn, as in black-thorn, but a local friend calls brambles 'thorns'. I am not sure if her 'thorns' is a catch-all name for bramble, blackthorn, hawthorn and whatever other thorns there are. If I did not hesitate to pounce on differences, to be the nosy collector, it would be interesting to know about those thorns, Somerset speech being a fugitive thing.

∾

The next day I borrowed a copy of Alfred Watkins's *The Old Straight Track* from Langport Library. It is the book in which Watkins sets out his ideas, or as he would have it, discoveries, about ley lines. 'Ley lines' was his own term for the prehistoric tracks he was convinced were still there, traversing the land, marked by hilltops, standing stones and other such durable items. This was the book my guide, Robert Dunning, had suggested as worth a look when we were talking of the possible former track down from the top of the escarpment at Bowdens, past the wood and on to the river.

Opposite the title page of this recent edition is a photograph of Alfred Watkins (1853–1935) looking like his near contemporary, Sigmund Freud. In his introduction, Robert Macfarlane is courteous towards Watkins, at the same time as dismissing his ideas as 'thoroughly wrong'. Nevertheless, not only did some people believe in ley lines and enjoy looking for them, the lines went on to gather more meanings, of mystical energy, and more believers in the 1960s and 70s. There are Ley Line Hunters still, with a website included within *The Megalithic Portal*.

Alfred Watkins was the son of a Herefordshire miller and brewer, who required him to contribute to the family firm rather than receive any higher education. Years passed in which he developed the business and exercised his spare intelligence with photographic innovation and antiquarianism, before he received his 'rush of revelations' on 30 June, 1921.

He was in Blackwardine, with a map. First on the map, then on the ground, a series of ancient sites linked themselves up in a straight line before his eyes. He was sure it could not be coincidence; it must be that straight tracks had been made between noticeable features in the landscape, so that travellers could find their way. These features being ancient, it followed that the tracks were too.

Three months later, Watkins presented his findings to The Woolhope Naturalists' Field Club. The 'Field' part of its name refers to field trips, and it was out of doors that Watkins directed the club members on that September day, so that they could see some alignments with their own eyes. Then he showed them lantern slides in the club's rooms in the Hereford Free Library and Museum.

Being a photographer was a help to Watkins as he assembled his evidence. From the photographs in the book it is not always easy to see what he means, though they form an expressive record in themselves. They did not, however, convince all his fellow club members, and nor did his first book. Certain that he was right, he set out to amass more evidence for his longer book, *The Old Straight Track*, 1925, the recent addition of which I now had to hand.

I wish I had left reading Robert Macfarlane's thoughtful, interesting essay till the end. Having read it first, to go on to hear Watkins's engaging voice, bubbling with excitement about his straight tracks, felt awkward. It was like being at a party, appearing to listen to a cordial, loquacious old guest, while already primed not to believe a word he says. Or at least, to be picking up on different things from those intended; on the atmosphere of another era, for instance, when business and culture were still local, when the prominent people of a city could feel in charge of their own world.

Watkins, a wealthy, intelligent, self-taught man, seems at once confident and diffident. Perhaps because he was not given any further education, he sympathised with women, trying in vain to get the Woolhope Club to change the rules and admit them as full members. Recently, the Society of Ley Hunters set up a stone in his honour at the Blackwardine crossroads. Few long-dead scholars inspire that sort of recognition. His name is still known now because of his imagination. Plenty of theories are wrong, some do harm, this one seems only to have given interest and pleasure.

As anticipated, *The Old Straight Track* had brought me no nearer to knowing if the track from my wood to the road was part of an older one from Aller Hill to the River Parrett. When I spoke to Doreen, Ted's widow, about it, she remarked, 'It could be, because nobody owns it.' This unexpected circumstance emerged when Philip, her son, was seeking permission to convert the sheds to a dwelling.

Ted had thought that he owned half the width of the track, with the farmer of the arable field owning the other, and whoever owns Sugg's Orchard having a right of way along it. That is what he told me and I never thought to question. Now it seems there is nothing in writing about the track at all.

Philip has since told me that when he was a boy, growing up in the white cottage near the section of track once known as 'Lower Road', it did indeed go somewhere. Currently it comes to an end near a big poplar, with rhines (ditches) blocking any approach to the river. Philip recalls a path proceeding for a bit before turning right, back towards Aller. The Ordnance Survey map of 1901 confirms this, in the form of 'Misbrook Drove'. I was sorry to see that it shows no onward path to the river.

As I was beginning to appreciate, maps and records sometimes contradict both local knowledge and what one would like to have been the case. I want the track to have led from hilltop to river because there is something satisfyingly complete in that idea. But tracks only go where people need, or needed, them to go.

Alfred Watkins not only imagined tracks, he pictured their users too, including prehistoric engineers and pedlars of salt, making their straight ways across country. I had not gone so far as to think who would want to walk down from Bowdens to the Parrett. The 1901 map does, however, mark a towpath along that stretch of river. The Parrett leads to the Bristol Channel and was, to some extent still is, navigable. So there it is, a possible use for the possible track; by taking it, travellers could begin a journey to destinations across the globe.

Indeed I can just picture the little ploughboy of popular song, whistling *o'er the lea* (the one we are to forget because he is going to do so well for himself). He is on his jaunty way down Aller Hill to seek his fortune, past the elm and field maple hedgerow, across into Lower Road, on down to the river, ready to hail the next coal barge returning to Bridgwater . . .

In antiquity, a divine stag came each springtime and cleared the spring with his horns until the water began to flow . . .

from Border, by Kapka Kassabova

It is because I like the sound of him that I have borrowed that mythic stag, transporting him from the mountains of Thrace to the lowlands of Somerset. Where stags also roam, although the chance that one of them could be behind the flowing of the spring water in the wood had not previously struck me. Instead, it was the suggestion that the water comes underground from the Mendip Hills that had taken root in my imagination.

As with the idea of the track, it was during a casual conversation that I had first heard of this possibility. I am unsure who mentioned it, but Mr Scriven did say that the water in the pond was unusually pure. 'Was' is the word, murky is more like it now.

In the summer of 2017 I had been pulling out armfuls of bur reed, which had arrived of its own accord and was clogging up what was left of the open pond water. Two unexpected things became noticeable; there were no water creatures, like shrimps, wriggling in the mud that came up with the roots, as there would have been a few years before, and a silver ring on my finger had gone black. It had been shiny, had often been in that water before and come out again shiny.

For some time there had been reason to fear that all was not right with the waste system further up the hill, and more recently the willows have been overshadowing the pond and shedding leaves into it. I thought that pollution, or lack of light, might be causing problems.

Accordingly, late on an August afternoon I took a one-litre sample of the pond water to Somerset Scientific Services for testing. It was in a transparent plastic bottle and looked like weak, bitty black tea. As with the Heritage Centre, the Scientific Services building is situated in unscholarly surroundings, perched on the edge of an industrial estate. However, within it a cloistered calm seemed to reign, the result, said the friendly boss, of my having arrived just before the Bank Holiday.

He shook the water in its bottle, observed that it did not appear to contain detergent (no froth), smelt it, said he had smelt much worse, and took it away. I forget if I tried out on him ideas about pure water from Mendip, but we talked of sewage, the pond, the silver ring, sulphur, missing shrimps and how he had loved living in London. Then I paid £48 and left.

When the analysis of the water came back, parts of it were incomprehensible to one who has never learnt any chemistry, but the comments box was clear . . . 'These results show that this water as received is a clean environmental water with no signs of any contamination from any leaking sewage tanks'.

While good in itself, this news made me regret having mentioned sewage, because the pond lies quite a way west of where the sewage used to escape. I should have confined the conversation to tarnished silver and absent water shrimps. At least it did seem as though trying to get more oxygen back into the pond was a better idea than worrying about pollution.

This episode had not thrown light on the Mendip question, and may have set a precedent. Pursuing the very pure water story has produced more enjoyable asides than firm conclusions, which is perhaps fitting, since the Mendips (or simply 'Mendip' as they are often called locally) are a very romantic line of hills. They stand above the former Avalon Marshes, their limestone hollowed into fantastical caves by underground water, with the bones of mammoth, bison, bear, rhinoceros and other creatures no longer associated with Somerset preserved in their depths.

As I began to circle the idea of the spring water, something dawned upon me. It was that the arrow-filled diagram everyone educated in Britain must sometime have copied, of rain falling, making its way to the sea, getting evaporated into clouds, being blown inland, then falling again, represents most of what, barring divine stags, I know about how water behaves. The diagram does not go into detail about the underground movement of water, or how springs work.

Something I did know was that the city of Wells lies below the Mendips and that water from them comes up in the Bishop's Palace Gardens. Wells also lies between Langort and Bath, where my brother, Martin, and sister-in-law, Louise, live, so we sometimes meet there, as we did on a changeable mid-March day.

Blustery rain clouds were just being swept away to reveal a sky of pure blue as we left the café and walked towards the Palace Gardens. Four elderly volunteer gardeners were trundling barrowloads of spent mushroom compost to spread on the many flower beds. The compost was a bright red/brown. As each load fell on the darker earth and the gardeners raked it around the fresh green shoots, it looked as though they were painting. As the gardeners in *Alice in Wonderland* painted the roses, so these were painting the dark soil.

The ponds with the welling-up water are in a far part of the garden, with a layout of sluices, channels, bridges. A noticeboard tells of how green dye was introduced to an underground river via a swallet up in the Mendips. When the water welled up green in the Palace Gardens pond, it proved that the source was, as had already been thought, the hills above the city.

Pleasing as this experiment was to read about, it sounded a tricky one to imitate. On our way out of the Palace grounds we admired the American Black Walnut. It was still in its leafless, blackest mode, but budding with promise.

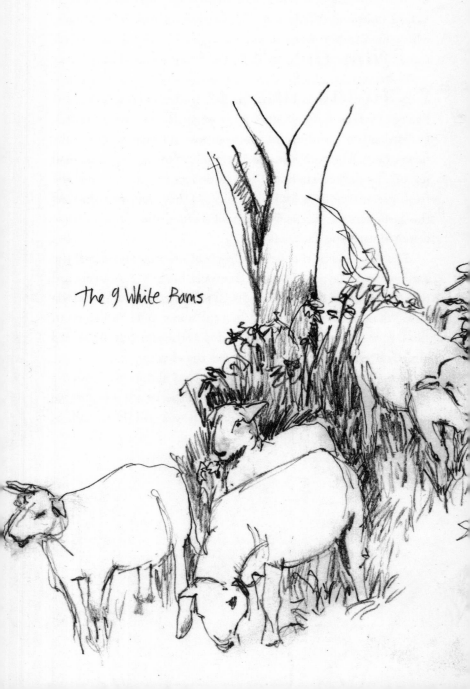

the 9 White Rams

From the Vernal Equinox
to the Summer Solstice

In April, I open my bill . . .

From a children's rhyme about cuckoos by Jane Taylor, 1783–1824

Kingcups, & reflections of willow in the pond   March

SOMETIME AROUND THE EQUINOX A BIG ash tree came
down, in what I now think of as the Disputed Territory of
the wood. Its roots were upended above the mapper's line
of stakes but most of the trunk and branches had fallen below
it, that is, into the can of worms. Part of the rough path Steve
had cut, so that the other landowner and I could walk round the
staked perimeter (to arrive, as I had hoped, at an agreement) was
now lost beneath a mashed tangle of branches. No harm, since the
landowner did not want to walk round with me anyway. Picking
a way back into undisputed territory felt better, like shutting a
door on trouble, even if all it was doing was putting it off.

The wind was tempestuous when I went looking for props
to support one of the old apple trees. The leaning tree, so one
expert thought, could be Warner's King, an old cooking apple.
It is described by different stockists as 'large pale greenish-yellow
fruit, splendid reliable cropper', 'green and sour', 'popular in
Victorian England, acid flavour' and so forth. These descriptions
fit quite well, except that only one mentions the colour pink, and

this tree's fruit is quite rosy. In my mind it has remained the Hermit's Apple, named for a folly made out of sticks that once stood behind it.

Andrew, who has done a lot of work in the wood over the years, had supported the leaning trunk with a T shaped prop. As time has passed, both have been slanting down more and more, engaged in a kind of slow motion tango. Encouraged by the example of the original Bramley's Seedling tree, I was hoping to help them hold up for a while longer. What with the wind howling and the gallant rooks cawing as they were tossed round their nests, it felt properly wild. Getting in under the muddle of low apple branches, I pushed in two props. In truth, it was more of a gesture than anything really secure. There are those who think that trees are open to sympathetic gestures; a pleasing, if doubtful idea.

Later, with rain and darkness added to wind, snowy-haired drivers were creeping round the green by Curry Rivel Church, looking for parking spaces. We were going to a concert. Inside, the sounds of harp, viola and flute were gentle enough to allow the drumming of the rain to join in. A bat flitted out from the organ loft for a moment, then flitted back.

In the interval of these concerts I like to help with the drying up, for the company. On this occasion, it led to an agreement with Catherine Mowat (botanist, not snowy-haired) that she would come and survey the wild plants at the wood, and also keep an eye/ear out for the birds. So that was an advance.

The next afternoon, early in the journey to London, a dramatic double rainbow promised repeated crocks of gold at every gate and tree.

ॐ

Waiting back in London was a card from the historian, Robert Dunning, about Sugg. Robert's comment, on having looked at the Aller Parish Registers, was 'the results might make the bones of a novel, but hardly a family history'. A quick look at the typed entries he enclosed made it easy to see why. People called Sugg, or Sugge, seemed to die much more often than marry or be baptised, some were even buried at the same time.

It looked as though it would be a sad novel, set between 1720 and 1780. For all that, how exciting to have real Suggs to think about. The following day I tried to make sense of their names and dates. Assuming that they were members of the same family, it was hard to be sure who belonged to which generation.

Other things inched forward, including sending Catherine information for her forthcoming botanical survey. And there was a visit I had long wished to make, to see Ron Scamp and his daffodil fields in Falmouth. This year of finding out more was the spur to doing so.

As well as breeding new daffodils, Ron Scamp has built up a collection of historic ones, varieties often developed before 1900. Many of them have an unshowy elegance, with their long slim leaves blending into the grass, making them look at home in a semi-wilderness. White Lady, Lucifer, Bath's Flame, Compressus, Mrs R. O. Backhouse and Barrii Conspicuus are among those varieties that Ron has supplied and are now sprinkled about the wood. The names of the last two recall luminaries of the nineteenth-century world of daffodil breeding; Mrs Backhouse and Peter Barr.

Years had slipped by since I met Ron at the Bath Spring Show, then posted him two bulbs from Ted's orchard. Ron identified them as a Leedsii, another variety to add to his collection. Edward Leeds (1802–1877) was at work earlier than Mrs Backhouse or Peter Barr. He is described by Noel Kingsbury in his book,

Daffodil, as an underappreciated pioneer of daffodil breeding, who nearly gave up because no one seemed interested. Luckily a few people were, so his collection, 'growing by thousands, almost wild', was not lost.

Ron's company is called 'Quality Daffodils'. I noticed on the website that Ron's name had been replaced by his son's, Adrian, so was afraid I might have left it too late to arrange a visit. Back came Adrian's reply, all was well, his father was retired but still working, so I was to make a date with him.

∾

It was not until April that I next saw the wood. A gloomy day had opened to sunshine by the time two young deer looked down from the top of the track, held their pose for a second, then bounded off into the trees.

There was one thing I wanted to check straight away, because of a recent dream. While not really believing it, I was anxious to see that the wooded slope above the boundary walk had not been bulldozed.

In the dream, trees lay fallen to either side and there, emerging from the churned earth was a track, of the very sort Alfred Watkins would have loved. It was paved with dark stone, neatly laid, straight as he could have wished, with a wall to one side. My dream self might have loved it too, if only it had been in a different place. Instead, it was not where I wish my old track to have been, and the question of who had caused the bulldozing hung in the air.

So in waking life it was a relief to find the boundary walk as I had left it, except that everything was greener and livelier, with more birdsong than before. 'White Lady', the daffodil that Ron Scamp once described to me as 'an old warhorse', was in full swing on its long stems, looking more graceful than a warhorse, and kingcups were in flower in the pond. There would have been bigger ones in the marsh if only some creature had not eaten them. Behind the Rollalong garden brambles were forcing a leggy old forsythia forward, which in turn was leaning over the wildish shrub roses and late narcissi. The brambles are unimpressed by the pretensions of the word 'garden', but I like that forsythia and do not want the brambles to have things all their own way.

The forsythia is the child of one that was already old in 1972, when we took over the London house in which I still live. Its pale yellow flowers are sparsely spread along wandering stems, perhaps more as the wild Chinese ones were when Robert Fortune collected the plant in the 1840s, and not like the newer, brighter, stubbier ones. Its parent in London died, seemingly of exhaustion, so I lectured myself not to let this one go. The cherry and pear blossom were looking perfect. A crescent moon was rising as I walked back down the track.

. . . *buried in wool only*

Soon I was back in the Somerset Heritage Centre in pursuit of Sugg, with kind Robert Dunning across the room with his vellum pages of priests' names. The original parish records are kept safe, not given out for everyone to thumb through. Instead, they have been digitised. Rather than the feel of crumbling pages and whiff of damp, the sensory experience is of sitting at a computer without, as at home, being able to fidget and get comfortable. Still, there is the backlit screen to help with the reading.

One thing that surprised me among the blotches and tatters and occasional pristine pages all faithfully scanned, was how often the handwriting changes. Crimped up, brown and forward-falling one moment, open and flowing the next, it looked as though in eighteenth-century Aller no one wanted to keep the job of recording baptisms, marriages and burials for long. Or maybe they, clerks, clergymen or whoever they were, did not live to fill a whole register with their handwriting. The Sugg family, if it was a family, was certainly not long-lived.

There they were, frequently dying and being wrapped 'in wool only' for their burial, with mention of affidavits written to confirm the use of wool. A few days before Christmas, 1736, 'Thomas, Anne and Peggy Sugge were all three buried'. I had already looked in vain for gravestones with the name Sugg in Aller churchyard, which is set on a slight rise above an expanse of low fields near the river. It may be much as it was in the 1700s, making it all too easy to imagine a bleak December day there, with the parson and a few others burying three children together. The baptismal dates suggest that they were children.

I asked Robert about 'in wool only'. He said that the wool industry had been doing badly, so legislation came in to protect it. Corpses should be shrouded in nothing but wool, to the annoyance of those who could afford linen or silk. It seems unlikely that the wool industry would have benefitted much from the amount of cloth it took to wrap the three Sugg children. Picturing that December day, and whoever had had to stand at the graveside, it struck me that wool might have looked a shade warmer than linen or silk, as the bundles were put in the earth. Because I was assuming, and Robert confirmed, that they would not have been in coffins. He remarked, in commendation of record-keeping, how good it is that people who lived so long ago, who were probably poor and obscure, have not completely vanished. We know that they lived, even if that is all we know about them.

Needless to say, I would like to know more about Sugg than that. For instance, if your name appears on records of land allocation, were you really poor? The recorded owners and occupiers of land are, however, sometimes different people. Part of what is now the wheat field appears as Sugg's Hill on the 1838 map, when neither owner nor occupier were called Sugg, so I did not feel confident about Sugg and his landholdings. Although that Sugg was a 'he' does seem a safe bet.

There is something about the research room of the Heritage Centre that gives me a headache. It is big, well-appointed and staffed by helpful people, so I conclude that the failing, probably to do with eyes screwed up, is mine. But on parting with Robert that day I was inclined to think the failing was Sugg's, for being elusive. So I announced that I had had enough of looking for him. At which Robert said gently, 'Really?' with an expression that suggested, 'Giving up already?'

Only a few days later, something odd happened. Stuck to a lamp post along Bow Street, Langport, appeared a blue-and-white label with, in printed letters 'Hello my name is', then handwritten in black felt-tip, 'SUG' followed by a graffiti-like squiggle. This greeting appeared where I could hardly miss it, when walking from the cottage to the car park. It stayed there for months, gradually weathering away.

Robert's look of surprise and Sug's timely salutation did the trick. It was too early to give up pursuing the one whose name had become attached to the land now in my care. As I sat in the cottage garden in unseasonably hot weather, trying to draw together what could be said about the Sugg family, I realised there were other questions still to be answered, for instance, if there were earlier or later Aller Parish records than those I had seen, or any Suggs still living locally. In both cases, there were.

I drafted a letter to the four people listed under Sugg in the Taunton and District telephone book, then thought better of it. My own family can hardly remember back to the 1860s, let alone to 1784, when Judith Sugg was buried in Aller. Unless the later parish registers recorded any more Suggs, it seemed unfair to be pestering people.

A further look at the registers yielded clusters of Suggs in other parts of Somerset but no more in Aller. After Judith's burial, the name fades out. When John Sugg married Anna Maria Lockyer in April 1718 (three hundred and one years almost to the day before I sat thinking about them) he may have been an incomer to the village. Lockyer is a name recurring throughout the registers, and still current in the area.

Although Robert's warning that the entries would make a better basis for a novel than a family tree still rings in my ears, I did get the dates to cohere into a sequence. It assumes that all the Suggs belonged to the same family. Though it may be quite different from what actually happened, here is a version of their story . . .

On 22 April, 1718, Anna Maria Lockyer married John Sugg. A year later, their son, John, was baptised, followed in June 1721 by their daughter, Ann. Ann's baptism, however, cannot be imagined as joyful, as her mother, Anna Maria, was buried on the very same day. Two years later, Thomas, the son of John and Elizabeth Sugg, was baptised. So let us guess that Elizabeth had married the widowed John, and taken on Anna Maria's children.

Next, in 1727, John Sugg was buried. As William, the son of John and Elizabeth Sugg was baptised four years later, the John who was buried is more likely to have been the eight-year-old boy, Anna Maria's son, than the adult John Sugg.

Maybe the good fairy hovered over William Sugg's cradle, fending off the illnesses of childhood, because only his baptism is recorded. In Aller, at least, he does not seem to have been married or buried, so he could have grown up and moved away. His younger sister, Peggy, had no such good fortune. She was baptised, then buried 'in wool only' in the same year, 1733, having lived for eight months. A second Peggy, born two years later, was scarcely any luckier.

Within little more than a year, Elizabeth, William's mother, was dead, in the middle of what must have been a desperate year. In Aller as a whole, four or five burials were recorded in 1734 and 35, but in 1736 and 37 the number leapt up to twenty-four.

It has not needed modern medical knowledge for people to know that an airy, uphill spot is a healthier place to live than down in the feverish marshes. Aller has hillside, but the river runs only a field or so from the church. The inhabitants must have come to some accommodation with the mosquitoes, the debilitating agues and recurrent shivering (probably caused by malaria) to go on living there at all, although Ralph Cudworth, a seventeenth-century rector, was keen to leave. As he wrote in 1618, 'The air is very bad . . . so I have often been in danger of death by reason of agues, etc., which make me desirous to remove.'

Which he did. Ralph Cudworth was one of the many rural clergymen over the centuries who have been driven to despair by lack of congenial, educated company. Or if not to despair, to nature study, or horticulture, or scholarship. Cudworth pursued the latter by taking up a post in Cambridge.

Whatever illness struck the village in 1736, it appears to have been exceptional. It was on 19 December of that year that Thomas, Anne and Peggy Sugg were 'all three buried'. Thomas, if he is the one baptised in 1723, would have been thirteen, Anne (assuming she is the same person as Ann) would have been fifteen, while the second Peggy was only one.

After 1736, the record would seem to leave John Sugg a widower again, alone with his five-year-old son William, except that another 'daughter of John Sugge', whose first name and baptism are not recorded, died in 1739. Poor shadowy girl, so much the more lost for being without a name . . . Then in 1748, John Sugg married Judith Hayward and, six years later, their daughter was baptised.

Only a year later, in 1755, John Sugg was buried. If he really was the same one who had married Anna Maria Lockyer in 1718, he was probably in his fifties, and died leaving a wife, Judith, a twenty-four-year-old son, William, and this infant daughter, also Judith. After that, there is only one more entry in the parish record, Judith Sugg's burial in February, 1784. She could have been the mother or the daughter.

Although this story is speculative, I must admit to having become quite keen on John Sugg, who had had enough about him to attract three wives. Not that that may mean much in terms of personal allure, since young women had so little choice. By marrying they risked dying in childbirth, but to remain single, if an option at all, left open the door to disrespect, and still the chance of dying in childbirth. The folk songs Cecil Sharp collected are full of girls betrayed and babies abandoned.

It may be that Anna Maria, Elizabeth and Judith, who all married John Sugg, were not as poor as they would have been without a man whose surname was attached to pieces of land. Looking on the bright side, John Sugg could have been the handsome stranger new to the village, putting the girls in a flutter, offending the lads they had known from childhood, getting on with acquiring property, planting apple trees, still being marriageable as a widower.

So I am inclined to like John Sugg, and hope that he is my Sugg, of Sugg's Orchard, Sugg's Hill, Sugg's Acre, working the same heavy soil that I now know, occasionally straightening up to glance across the miles of moorland, or to hear the song thrush. I wish there were not so many years between his last appearance in Aller and the name appearing on the Enclosure Act map, but there it is. And there, unless anything else turns up, I shall have to leave him.

Tossing their heads in sprightly dance

From Daffodils by William Wordsworth

Second only to snowdrops, daffodils are the flowers I most wish to see establishing themselves in and about the wood. The excitement of daffodil breeding in the last two centuries in this country has been giving way to the Dutch mastery of the bulb trade, but in Cornwall it is still alive.

Falmouth, where Ron Scamp grows his daffodils, is a long way from Langport, so I got up early and went by train from Taunton. It felt right to be going on a daffodil trip by rail, as the Cornish spring flower trade was all tied up with the spread of the railway. Fantastic numbers of daffodils were grown and transported to London and other big towns in the glory days of the trade, which lasted till after the Second World War.

There is still a good number of daffodils coming up to London every year, by road. When I asked the polite if somewhat surprised man who answered the Great Western Railway Customer Helpline, it took him a while to establish among his colleagues that no, daffodils are no longer carried by train from the West Country.

I had earlier wondered if Falmouth still had a station but it was all right, it has three. The first you come to along the branch line from Truro is Penmere Platform, where Ron had said he would meet me.

Alighting (the sole passenger to do so) into this lovingly kept place, its old-fashioned cream and brown paintwork fresh, its flower beds well-tended, was a touch disconcerting. It was not like happening upon a bustling period re-enactment or film set, no one was dressed as a pre-war porter or holding back tears after a brief encounter . . . instead, the place was sunny, pretty, quiet and deserted, as though becalmed in a pocket of time. I scurried away down the sloping path in search of Ron. There he was in the tiny car park, the recently honoured Master Grower of the Royal Horticultural Society Cardiff Spring Show.

Any grower would be pleased to be appointed an RHS Master, but as we skimmed along in the car, up and down between wooded banks full of daffodils, I began to appreciate the dedication and resource that had gone into the making of this particular Master. Ron, a war-time baby with his step-father's surname, did not make it sound as though there had been much to cushion him on his way to becoming a master grower. As a boy, picking daffodils for his uncle, he came to love them. He wanted to work with them, raising new varieties, conserving old ones, selling bulbs. Gradually, by doing two jobs at once, he got there.

We turned off the lane on to a track leading to some former rough farmland Ron now owns. There is a large packing shed, which they built themselves, a drying shed, bays for machinery,

Narcissus 'White Lady'
in rough grass

an area for bringing on new hybrids. Ron and his son, Adrian, had only just returned from the Cardiff Show, so the floor space of the packing shed was crammed. Big pots of daffodils were still looking handsome, one variety, white with an orange cup, was called 'Notre Dame'. After the fire that had so recently roared through the cathedral in Paris, I found that a striking name. Ron was more concerned to impress upon me that the shed was usually much tidier than this.

He was shy of having photographs taken inside which I first thought, wrongly, might be to do with craftsmen's secrets. It was only because of what he saw as the muddle. Being run as a tight ship, I was beginning to gather, was a key element of the success of 'Quality Daffodils'. With Adrian, we started discussing the intricacies of loading, transporting, unloading and displaying show plants.

I knew that they were not exaggerating these hazards, simply from the experience of taking children's exhibits to a local flower show. The description of how Ron and Adrian make the blooms safe for long journeys was further evidence of the tight ship, or van. As was the question of labelling.

Not all daffodil bulbs look the same, but when you are harvesting hundreds of different varieties from open windy ground, secure labelling comes into its own. So, in this case, does the sort of frugality only really comprehensible to those who remember war-time and post-war shortages. The tail end of which I can, just, recall. That, and the fragility of labelling in the wood, made me appreciative of Ron's recipe for a durable label . . .

First, find some old wooden fence palings. Cut into lengths of about half a metre, paint the top half with white emulsion, write with waterproof black marker, then varnish. Ron showed me baskets of these labels, not thrown in any old how, placed alphabetically, 'Larkhill', 'Lemonade', 'Lemon Spice'. Since we are speaking of daffodil varieties, there were several more names starting with 'lemon'.

Experts recommend taking the dead flowers off daffodils, to save them the effort of producing seed. But as I want them to naturalise, I have wondered about this advice. In the wild, up in the mountains of Spain or Portugal where daffodils are at home, no one would be deadheading. The bulbs would be spreading through 'clumping up' or seeding.

I asked Ron what he thought of letting daffodils go to seed. He said it takes years for seedlings to get anywhere, the best way is to split up their clumps. So naturalizing (a practice popularised by Peter Barr, the Victorian daffodil breeder) is not quite as natural as it sounds.

Anyone who breeds new varieties of daffodil is accustomed to waiting. The seedlings, crosses of this or that parent, nurtured and fed, will bulk up in four or five years, to flower after six. Then you see if any good has come of the wait, and bring on the promising ones. As Ron showed me some of his seedlings it became clear why, in retirement, he is still working. With an expressive sweep of the hand, he showed boxes of them . . . the gesture said, they need him, they might be something special, they are not letting him go.

The main daffodil fields are among those belonging to a local farmer, which is good for the rotation of crops. It means that the bulbs can get a change of soil and, with luck, leave their pests and diseases behind. Ron took me up to the fields they are currently using, which stretch towards the headland over the sea, interspersed with hedges and trees. In the foreground are rows upon rows of daffodils, an undulating quilt of green, yellow, white and creamy stripes.

This was in the second half of April, when even in normal years the season would be advanced. This year, with its mild winter, strong winds and hot sun, the heavy loam soil was looking dry. I was squeaking in late, but there were still enough bulbs in flower to make the whole prospect thrilling.

The rows are planted in alphabetical order, the historical varieties mixed in with the others. Except, Ron said, for the miniatures and for rows of 'Ron's Rainbow Mixture', the splendour of which he regarded rather regretfully for a moment, 'Look at that . . . we don't charge enough for them!' Then he departed for an hour, saying I was to enjoy myself and pick a bunch to take home.

Apart from the company of larks singing high up out of sight, and glimpses of the sea in the distance, I was alone with the daffodils. Ron had said, of seeing wild ones up in the snowline in Northern Spain, 'You're in heaven'. Being let loose among cultivated ones in Cornwall might not be quite so transporting, but nearly.

The ex-fence-post labels were out in force. By walking up and down the rows, making notes, taking pictures, the idea was to learn more about the historical varieties. However, because they were sorted alphabetically, not by period, I kept coming across ones I might have skipped in the catalogue. It was exciting to find that I could leave off pure simplicity and be enchanted by the scented pink and cream ruffles of decidedly showy, often more recent, varieties.

Showiness is a quality nurserymen need in their plants, since awards and prizes matter in the horticultural trade. Ron says some of his fellow growers are bewildered that he should bother with collecting and propagating old varieties. Though they may have won prizes years ago, they are never going to win them now . . . to which his response is, 'I like 'm'. It is also true that there is a market for them. There was an upsurge of interest in the 1980s that has kept going since, fed by the fact that some growers had never given up on the old varieties and had been making collections. Even now, clumps of bulbs are still to be found in old gardens, even in hedgerows, coming up year after year, ready to be rediscovered, pondered over, identified.

Ron came back to check on me, saying I was welcome to stay longer. If only I had felt up to taking in more, there were swathes I had not yet seen, but the thought of a break in a coffee shop was nudging its way in. Also, a friend had sent a message recommending a ferry ride while in Falmouth, so that is what I chose to do. Ron took me to the quay, before setting off on another assignment. If what I had seen of him that day was typical, his wife's reservations about his version of retirement are easy to understand.

∽

Easter is a moveable feast but even so, it could usually be relied upon to be cold. Although it was a pleasure to be sitting outside as though it were summer, it also felt wrong, especially with the news of wildfires burning on Ilkley and Marsden Moors. While nothing as alarming was happening in the wood, the ground was already cracked.

An unplanned conjunction of visitors happened in the wood on Easter Saturday. Three generations of my brother's family were gathering branches to make a den. The two boys would have preferred to be climbing or making a tree house, but the trees are mostly too young or too old for that. Cakes, sticking plasters, creams for stings and bruises were all in readiness in the Rollalong. Chairs were set out for Martin and Louise, my brother and sister-in-law, from which to observe the construction, once enough wood was assembled. All was cheerful as we scoured the hazel wood, making piles.

Below us, a woman appeared wearing a sunhat. She was carrying a clipboard and looking absorbed. At first I had no idea who she was, then she turned out to be Catherine, the botanist, whose message to say she was coming I had missed in the flurry of making lunch. In hindsight, I should have been cordial, offered tea, but not tried to engage with the botany of the wood. Instead, thinking that the family was having a good time and would continue to do so without me, I set off with Catherine to look at various plants she had noticed, including some growing in a small patch of 'unimproved' calcareous grassland.

In the context of wild flora, 'unimproved' land is good. It means that farmers have not got to it with fertilisers or allowed it to be overgrazed. I did have enough experience of botanists to know that what they get excited about is not necessarily the sort of plant to attract non-botanists. Such a one was *Plantago media*, beside which we knelt in appreciation up near the Hermit's Apple. It looked, unsurprisingly, like a plantain, with a rather mingy rosette of dark green, ridged leaves and, as yet, no upward growing stalks. I gathered that Catherine was taking the trouble to point it out because its presence indicated the desirable, unimproved nature of that patch of soil.

We then set off in various directions, including the marsh, where Catherine said that the handsome plant I dislike for its exuberant takeover is *Carex pendula*, pendulous sedge. The worst thing about it doing so well, not just in the marsh but also on top of clumps of primroses and snowdrops, is that I probably introduced it myself.

I can picture a friend, a native of Devon and former teaching colleague, tossing down a heap of plants brought from Devon to try in the school garden, saying, 'This is a tough old thing, it might work here, and maybe in your wood'. That tough old thing was pendulous sedge. It did survive in London, in an awkward rubbly border. But nothing like so well as it does in the damp lower reaches of the wood.

Catherine paused at a clump of bluebells outside the Rollalong, saying that it was a shame that the Spanish hybrids were moving in among the native ones and that I should not let them set seed. Later I took her advice, picking all the offending ones that were in flower. That afternoon, aware that it was a long time since I had attended to the family, I did not engage with her about the more complicated process that may be going on in that bed, where some of the bluebells actually look more like natives than when they were first planted there.

Louise called over, asking if she could put the kettle on, and where was the nettle-sting cream? By the time Catherine and I had said goodbye, she promising to write up a report, it was clear that the mood of the family party had changed. What had started as purposeful and energetic had turned into something between desultory and truculent, that even cake could do little to rescue. Louise had evidently been trying her best to keep things going, not least in the treatment of nettle stings.

The boys were no longer interested in the den, which their father was completing on his own. They had found a new way to amuse themselves, sitting in the wheelbarrow. There was only room for one of them at a time, with results on which we need not dwell. I decided against trying a diversion to the only tree that might be climbable, a far distant, lolloping dogwood, because the afternoon seemed irremediable. Irremediable that is, until after photos had been taken to show their absent mother, and they were back in the car, ready for the journey home. My last image is of them sitting peaceably together, each with headphones on.

Martin and Louise left soon afterwards, while I stayed to clear up. Then I sat down with a drink, looking at the den. If it had brought any pleasure I might have felt more kindly towards it.

Instead I took it apart, stowing the lengths of wood under the Rollalong. The fact is, I had invested some hope in that visit, because of the future. Keenly remembering how much nettle stings hurt young skin, I had not asked the boys to the wood before, but now they are long past infancy I had hoped they might love the place.

Instead, I had neglected them, they had had a disappointing time, their father had laboured on a hot afternoon when he might have preferred to be snoozing in the shade. They would all dislike the wood forever and not want anything to do with it after I am dead, and it was my fault. Or so it seemed, as I sat sipping stale sherry on the exact twentieth anniversary of my having taken on the wood.

The next day, again far too hot for Easter, I sat woefully reading the paper, admiring the Extinction Rebels, sorrowing over murdered Sri Lankans, worrying about wildfires, generally despairing. When the heat abated I went up to the wood.

There it was, its own self, with all its various fresh greenery steeped in a rosy glow. Beauty is in the eye of the beholder, so what I see as enchanting, others may regard as a scruffy, ill-kept pickle. Still, it was there in its own right, its many constituent parts getting on as best they may. I felt I should have more confidence in it, stop fretting about who does or does not love it.

∽

About this time, a friend showed me a photocopied and stapled memoir, *As I Remember . . .* by Pat Twiney, produced in 2014 when the writer was eighty-one. It tells the story of a girl, an only child, growing up on a smallholding on the Wiltshire/ Somerset border. It was remote enough that she did not know other children before going to school, so grew up with animals for company and a keen eye for plants. On leaving school she joined her parents on the smallholding (the memoir omits this, but she subsequently said that she would have preferred to stay on at school and become a librarian).

After the war, they were still working the smallholding in a traditional way. Bob the carthorse pulled the machinery, they used no artificial fertilisers . . . 'with such a rich variety of herbage the cattle did well and kept very healthy'. There are several observations like that, music to the ears of those disenchanted with 'improved' agriculture.

Brief, clear, unsentimental, Pat's memoir is a model. It remains very local (going to school in Frome and then Bruton is about the limit of it) but her remarks touch on things of wider interest; changes in farming, land ownership and use, community, roads, transport.

As anyone with a passing knowledge of rural life knows, vehicles, the state of the roads, transport in general, are vital topics. In youthful ignorance, I would despair of the country pubs to which I tagged along with my father, because the conversation was always about cars and roads. Now I understand that better.

Pat gives an example of rural pragmatism dating from before her own time. Speaking of a road that had been very wide before it was hardcored, she says, 'carts would simply drive around the ruts and potholes to avoid them and as it was very wet ground they made more ruts and potholes . . . and so the roadways grew wider and wider'. So wide, that when the hardcoring finally happened there were cultivable strips freed up on both sides. From her own early memory she recalls 'there were very few cars and each was known by its different engine noise. We only had to listen out to know who was driving by!'

Aller and Langport are about thirty miles to the west of where Pat is describing, so her memories may seem irrelevant to my wish to know about the wood's tracks and springs. But she gives such a strong sense of the ways things change, sometimes going for good, that it is like having a sensible voice in my ear, advising that, though the past may still be legible in the landscape, it may also not be, it may have vanished away.

In her account, woods get axed, allowing wild flowers and strawberries to spring up, then trees are replanted, cottages tumble down, some disappearing, some getting spruced up, lightning destroys a landmark monkey puzzle tree, hedges are torn out, family and neighbours come and go, a church becomes a dwelling place, the land of small farms gets put together.

Reading all this, I wondered if Aller might have its own memoir writers. They might not be as interested in paths and woods as Pat is, but the thought of what might be preserved in local memory was intriguing. Langport Library could offer a 'Knit and Natter' group, but not one for memoir-writing. Even by my elastic standards, knitting and nattering sounds an indirect avenue for research.

So I turned to Doreen, long a resident of Aller, to ask who in the village might have a good memory. Doreen thought they had all 'gone on', except for one whose memory might no longer be so good. Since first coming to Aller I had heard of this man, but never happened to meet him nor thought of trying to do so, until too late.

Even though no expert witness was forthcoming, my ears were now better tuned to who was related to whom, who had spent their childhood in Aller, then moved away. Something I have always liked about this area is that people may move, but often not very far. Unlike the name, Sugg, which comes and goes from the records inside a single century, several surnames recur for hundreds of years.

The links, through family, school, work, etc., that might strike other city dwellers as claustrophobic, seem to me a source of strength. Through such links I met Graham Lock, who had grown up and farmed in Aller when there were still eight local farms as opposed to two or three. Then, via Paradise (situated in this instance close by) he had moved to Huish Episcopi. He showed me old photographs, including one of the former Aller National School, now shut. In this 1950s picture, boys are out gardening in what looks like an idyllic scene, rose pergola and all. There are no girls at work in the garden. They may have had to stay indoors, knitting.

In May, I sing all day

May Day brought welcome news from the sheep-owner, Laura, that she would soon be putting in some 'nibblers'. By mid-May when I next saw it, the bottom of the track was fringed with the white lace of cow parsley; Queen Anne's Lace, it is also called. As I approached the gate to the wood, nine white rams trotted down to meet me on the other side. Once I was inside, they soon made clear who was the visitor, and an inadequate one for not having brought them anything tasty.

The boldest ram stamped his hoof when all I did was offer a fond greeting and speak of fresh grass. They soon huffed off, making their disapproval felt. That was the only time they did that. The next day they took no interest in my arrival, seeming to exhibit more intelligence than they are often given credit for.

As already mentioned, my fondness for sheep is not shared by many environmental campaigners, notably George Monbiot. In

aris foetidissima

Pyramidal Orchids
among the thistles,
docks & grasses
June

Turkish Iris

Feral, he says, 'Sheep farming in this country is a slow-burning ecological disaster, which has done more damage to the living systems . . . than either climate change or industrial pollution'. His horror of the state to which overgrazing by sheep has reduced the Welsh hills is well known, and easy to understand.

My hope is that having a few sheep in for a short time is different. Unlike squirrels, true delinquents, the rams were being quite good guests. To judge from the look of the place, they must have been in for a few days. Their pathways were already established and the long grass was getting shorter. Not short, not a velvety sward bejewelled with dainty flowers, such as I dream of. That may require a tame unicorn.

Elder trees and the medlar were full of their beautiful white flowers. Both fragrant, the elderflowers lacy and flat, the medlars more like single, pink tinged roses. Up near the cedars the double white lilac, Madame Lemoine, was looking and smelling its best. Like Mrs R. O. Backhouse of the daffodils, Madame Lemoine was not just a nurseryman's wife who had plants named in her honour. Sarah Elizabeth Backhouse and Marie Louise Lemoine were both active plant breeders.

When Victor Lemoine's eyesight was making it hard to do the necessary hand pollination, his wife, Marie Louise, was there with the right skills. At their nursery in Nancy they bred a range of plants (much as Kelway's Nurseries did in Langport in the same era). Several are called 'Madame Lemoine', but it is lilacs that come to mind at the sound of her name.

Because single flowers are better from the pollinators' point of view, more accessible and rewarding, there is now ambivalence about the project that excited so many nineteenth-century horti-culturalists, to make garden flowers bigger, more double. When those plant breeders set about their patient craft with fine brushes and tweezers, imitating and organizing the work that pollinating insects do spontaneously, insects were everywhere; a more normal preoccupation then might have been with how to kill them. We have since succeeded in doing so to such an alarming degree that thoughts have now had to turn to what suits a bee, a butterfly, a moth, or, less glamorously, a fly.

From the undergrowth on the way to the Rollalong a small rabbit popped up on a fallen log at the edge of the old burrows. It looked all right, if slow to go back down again. A rabbit corpse that had been lying by the gate to the hazel wood had gone. In the long grass by the silvery willow there was another one, with part of its abdomen missing. There never used to be rabbit corpses lying around.

One sad aspect of worrying about the state of the natural world is that everything starts to look wrong. I see a rabbit and immediately fear for its health, I look up at the patchy foliage around the nests in the ash trees and, instead of assuming that the leaves are not yet fully out, Ash Dieback is my first thought. As it happens, I am not yet aware of Ash Dieback in the wood, but it is certainly getting closer. At least the rooks were in fine form and voice, circling round their nests.

I took out the new, battery-powered strimmer. Compared with the old petrol machine with its starter rope, this one is a treat to use. I had been unsure if it was my arms or the old machine at fault, but it had become the devil to start. Dave Locke, mower expert, also had trouble with it, which was heartening.

The light Austrian scythe I bought after attending a scything course would have been the better, more 'green' choice. Sharpening its blade, however, is the sort of task I find very easy to put off. Truth to tell, it was disappointing that the scything course turned out to be so full of technicalities and precise skills. Even with sweet simplicity, it appears, there are still plenty of opportunities for getting things wrong.

So far, the new strimmer whirs gently into life without any hesitation, makes less noise than the petrol one, and keeps going as long as I want it to. It does not seem to emit anything bad, although there are questions over the making of batteries. None of that concerned me as I wove through the May evening, pleased to be restoring some order to the grass around the Rollalong. The sheep are not invited in to do it because they might fall into the zuggy pond and never get out again.

I tried to avoid the self-seeded clumps of sweet rocket, cow parsley, comfrey, and also the nettles with their leaves furled up, in case they had caterpillars pupating inside. Then some small creature made the grasses shiver as it took fright and plunged away. Maybe a mouse or a frog . . . I never saw it, but was fairly sure that it had got away with all its body parts intact. Still, that was enough for that session.

Rain was forecast. Rather than confront the 'electric gate' to take the young walnut tree a can of water, I just greeted it from afar, said goodbye to the rams and went home. By the next afternoon the partly eaten rabbit corpse had disappeared. On the shoulder of land below the Hermit's Apple, a rabbit was nibbling and lolloping about in the sun, looking normal. Then, a possibly connected sight, a fox trotted by, the first I have seen there for several years. However silly it is to take sides in nature's uncompromising struggles, I was pleased for the rabbit that the fox had arrived too late.

Most wool is now worth so little that Laura's sheep are of a 'labour-saving' breed, which means that there is no need to shear them, their wool just falls off. Wool is, however, used in expensive gardening products to deter slugs and snails, so I gathered some of the fallen pieces of fleece to try them in the mollusc-rich cottage garden. Underneath, the wool looks surprisingly different from the white fluffy stuff we are used to. It is clumped together into a tight yellow oily mesh, hard to pull apart and smelling rankly of lanolin. When placed on the garden beds, with an outer ring of wood ash, the fleece was neither pretty, nor alas, effective.

∾

Roger Dickey carried out his initial bird survey and sent the table of results. The format of this table (reproduced as an appendix) is probably standard, but its details struck me as very pleasing . . . as in, the waning gibbous moon on the clear, cold night before, and that Roger had started at 9 a.m. on a cloudless, slightly windy day and continued for two hours. During that time he recorded the presence of twenty-one species, many of them busy carrying food, being juvenile, singing or calling, two roosting, one feeding, one hunting.

This is the first time, to my knowledge, that anyone has recorded the birds in the wood, so it is uncertain whether the list represents a tragedy of decline, an encouraging record of survival, or something in between. From the tone of much I have read, notably Ian Newton's scholarly *Farming and Birds*, the likelihood is of tragic loss, and Roger confirms 'there has undoubtedly been a decline in species and populations over the last ten years'. He adds that his one visit does not amount to a proper survey, so it is insufficient evidence. Still, twenty-one species in two hours sounded exciting to me (with two more, marsh tit and garden warbler, seen by Catherine Mowat a month before, and noted because they are scarce).

Some of the species were familiar, like robin, wood pigeon, blue tit. I was still not quite adjusted to my 'crows' up in the ash trees actually being rooks. Not that I have anything against rooks, but had understood that they have baggy thigh feathers and a bald patch above the beak, which these do not appear to have . . . 'Juveniles don't', says Roger. The clinching fact, though, is about how they nest; crows singly, rooks in colonies. Roger also said that listening is a way of telling them apart.

According to the *RSPB Book of British Birds*, the call of a rook is a loud 'kaah' while the call of a crow is a harsh croaking 'craah'. Something alliterative seems to be going on here . . . rook kaah, crow croaking craah. Anyway, they are rooks, and Roger counted twenty-five of them, mainly juveniles.

He had seen a spotted flycatcher feeding at the edge of the wood, which he recorded with a query about its territory. The rate of loss of spotted flycatchers since 1970, as noted by Ian Newton in *Farming and Birds*, is 87 per cent. So, to see one at all sounds good, but how much more so it would have been to see a pair, or if the single one had been 'carrying food', as were some of the four goldfinches, six chiffchaffs, seven great tits, three blue tits, six blackbirds, two chaffinches . . .

The name 'flycatcher' tells something of its trouble. If insect numbers have collapsed, a bird that eats very little else is at a disadvantage. Many of the species Roger recorded are better at spreading their bets, eating a mixture of things the wood can offer; insects, seeds, berries, worms, caterpillars, mammals, the eggs and young of others. Of blue tits, the RSPB book says, 'a brood of young needs between 600–1000 caterpillars a day'. No wonder the parent birds look preoccupied.

In his *Farming and Birds* I was struck by how often Ian Newton mentions the loss of nesting sites, as well as of food. The wood is full of trees in various stages of health and decay, and of thickets of thorn and bramble. Not only was I confident the birds would sort themselves out, the RSPB suggests that people who put up bird boxes should keep them clean; a job too far, I feel.

However, Roger says that the right sort of nesting box at the edge of the wood would certainly help the declining population of little owls. I do not know if there ever were little owls in the wood, but now that I look them up, the idea of helping them does seem irresistible. Not only for their enchanting Latin name, *Athene noctua*, and the fact that they are so very little, 'the size of a starling', but because the bird book also says that sometimes their nest sites can be in continuous use for at least twenty-five years (without, presumably, a human fussing over them).

So, I had better try. If they fail to arrive, like all those bugs and bees and hedgehogs who never booked into the 'hotels' we lovingly provided for them in the school garden, well, my aunt was sure that goodwill is a positive force in a troubled world . . .

Catherine Mowat sent her plant survey a few days later. She had divided it into different areas, wooded, grassy, pond, damp, with the plant names in English as well as Latin. There are more than a hundred of them. I had a good time looking up the unfamiliar ones, recognizing some from the illustrations, trying out their names, forgetting them again. The most unfamiliar to me, and therefore exciting, were the grasses, the bents and fescues and fogs, the sweet vernal grass, the annual meadow grass. Even if I have taken against a few of these for their tussocky habits, for instance, the ones I take to be cocksfoot or red fescue, it was still good to hear their names.

The report begins with Catherine's reading of the land and the uses to which it may have been put. Starting with 'the species noted do not indicate habitat of long-standing' she suggests that the grassland has either been fertilised, or intensively grazed, or shaded by scrub for many years. The scrub possibility is right, the grazing one may be, because I know that Mr Scriven did have 'beasts' drinking from the pond, but fertilisers other than dung are less likely.

She notes the hazel wood as an exception to the lack of 'long-standing', but it looks to her from the absence of ancient woodland indicator plants, like primroses or wild bluebells, as though some grazing has been going on in there too. Which is probably true. Andrew told me that, as a boy working after school for Mr Scriven, he had to carry water up there for the pigs. Primroses and wild bluebells would have been lovely, but I do relish the idea that wood pasture, the ancient practice that sounds so sensible and yet romantic when mentioned by Oliver Rackham or John Lewis-Stempel, still continued there almost until my time.

Catherine noted one ancient woodland indicator plant, spurge laurel (*Daphne laureola*). It grows here and there in the wooded parts, not quite as restlessly as the violets along the boundary walk, but still with a tendency to move about. It is evergreen and flowers in winter, with a faint fragrance. A plant near the hazels that seems to have escaped the pigs is false oxlip. I thought it was simply oxlip until being told that that was highly improbable in Somerset. Which Catherine confirmed, so I now acknowledge that this amiable flower is false. It keeps to one place, making a patch that can vary in size from year to year but not striking out into new ground.

For the love of them, here are some of the names from Catherine's list of plants that had been nameless to me before . . . false wood-brome, common mouse-ear, crested dog's tail, bristly ox-tongue, Yorkshire fog, thyme-leaved speedwell, madder, meadow vetchling, blunt-flowered rush, bittersweet. It is easy to see the point of botanical Latin but for warmth and imagery, I do prefer the common names.

∾

The last part of May stretching into June is a season I have come to recognise as the time when it feels the wood is all getting too much. Everything grows non-stop, the clarity of winter and spring, with its separate longed-for moments of budding, unfurling, blossoming, singing, gets overwhelmed by a great wave of green, much of it from nettles and thistles. Both are beautiful and beneficial in their way and a true 're-wilder' would think only well of them. But my practice inhabits a borderland between cultivation and wildness, where the rules are unclear. One thing that is clear, however, is that for young trees and plants you wish to do well, the wave of green needs some pushing back.

This particular year a degree of control was even more desirable, because of the 'Ebenezer Presents' talk I was to give in Aller in early June. From being a distant, nothing-to-worry-about prospect it was now the wolf speeding nearest the sledge. It was not so much the talk itself, it was the woodland walk that was like that flying wolf.

Practical things needed doing; the track and the paths being mown, and probably mown again, overhanging brambles cut back, the rabbit holes being marked (filling them in had been nothing more than a fantasy). For insurance purposes, a notice saying 'POND' needed to announce the pond. But at heart, I was more concerned that visitors would be disappointed that this place I had lyricised about was, in reality, a mess.

The standard set by such organizations as the National Trust or National Gardens Scheme is so high, health and safety so important, that people are unused to fence posts that wobble or grafted trees where the rootstock is outcompeting the desired growth. Inaudible were the wise words with which I had so lately bolstered myself, about trusting the wood to be its own place, regardless of what other people think.

∞

At the end of May, soon after the nine white rams had departed, I met Steve one fair morning at the top of the track. He was unpacking his car. As well as his strimmer and other sundries, he uncurled himself from under the hatchback to present a sturdy young oak tree growing in a pot. It was about half a metre tall, looked the picture of health, and came with a story attached.

Jack Fieldhouse was an artist and beekeeper who had lived near Bridgwater and died at a ripe age. At his funeral his son had handed out acorns to be grown in memory of his father. Jeremy Harvey, through whom I know Steve, was at the funeral and received an acorn. Although he and his wife have an interesting garden in Taunton, the oak tree would have grown too big for it. Hence, by an arrangement I had forgotten, Steve had brought the sapling in its pot.

People quite often want homes for scruffy seedling trees which they have been starving in small pots, so I have developed a thickish skin about them. But artists, beekeepers and sons who think of giving out acorns at funerals are not two a penny. Besides, the oak looked promising, so I welcomed it.

The day's agenda started with paths and overhanging brambles but after lunch I went prospecting for a suitable oak planting space. Gaps have opened in the outgrown hedgerow where the tall wych elm, much later than its common elm relations, has been dying of Dutch elm disease. The rootstock of both remains alive and sends up suckers, but I wondered if an oak tree might fit in between. However, what with fallen timber and a close, draped cladding of ivy, horizontal and vertical, it would have taken a lot of time and energy to clear a space.

Moving inwards to the path that leads up to Madame Lemoine and the cedars, I came to the site where my once-favourite old apple tree stood, defying time as it continued to grow on its hollowed-out trunk, propped by a big forked branch of elm. The elm prop, eaten by woodworm, was the first to fall, followed soon after by the apple. In vain I waited, hoping it might put down new roots. In 2015, near the hulk of the apple, friends and I planted a tulip tree, which has already grown quite tall.

It is hard to guess how well a tree will do, how much space you should leave it. In the climate we were used to, tulip trees and oaks both grow big. As things warm up, the tulip tree might feel more at home than the oak, but I could only assume that they would both need a fair bit of room. In which case, they will have to come to an agreement between themselves, shoulder to shoulder on one side but free to spread outwards everywhere else. With a changing climate there are many tree-planting 'if's to consider, when thinking ahead even as little as thirty years, because temperature and rainfall are so critical to trees. The more research funding is put into tree genetics and sustaining the biodiversity of woods, the better.

Reverting to the future of one oak tree, Steve dug the hole and banged in a stake. Yellow ropes of nettle root were criss-crossing the ground but in went the oak sapling with its earth from the pot, then its wire cage around it and the job was done. Steve seemed surprised that I had expected it to take longer. He has done plenty of planting in woodland near Crewkerne, and was on to the next task. I would have spent time digging up the nettle roots and the tap roots of dock from around the planting hole, to give the young tree a while longer before they all grew back. And I did spend time fetching a can of rainwater from the butt by the Rollalong, and watering it in.

To be given a tree in memory, even though the memory is of a man I never met, and then let it die would not be good, so I kept up the watering whenever there was a chance. So far, the young oak seems happy with its speedy planting. I am curious to see if the way I tend to take a ceremonious amount of time with each planting is unnecessary. Maybe both speedy and slow have their advantages . . . little as I like the image, there is usually more than one way of skinning a cat.

Steve went on working. By the time he left he had cleared the paths and sawn off a big dead hazel branch so that it would not fall on anyone. The hazel has bracket fungus, which is what made me think the dead branch might fall. Once it was gone the sawn stump looked sad, and more noticeable than had the whole dead branch. Steve had also cut back some elders, to give the flag irises more light. During this time I had meant to start marking the rabbit holes with black and yellow tape tied to sticks, but instead lay out on cushions, looking up at the twinkling willow leaves.

A few days earlier I had tripped on a hidden hole and lain flat out, gathering my wits. Once having decided that the strimmer and I were uninjured, there seemed no hurry to get up. Watching the whitest of clouds chase across a blue sky was the sort of pleasure I felt was worth taking more often. This time the sky was not so bright, more of a soft grey. The willow leaves were clear in outline, looking as though drawn with a fine pen, always moving but always distinct. They looked familiar . . . from cushion covers and wallpaper. Perhaps William Morris had lain out like this, before designing his 'Willow Bough'.

the Pond, marked for
insurance purposes ...

In June, I change my tune

Martin and Louise gave a party in Bath to celebrate their fiftieth wedding anniversary. It was impressive to see their loyal friends, no longer young, negotiating the steep steps of the back garden without coming to harm. The wood's rabbit holes, now marked, were unlikely to be any more hazardous than those steps. The day of their wedding fifty years before had been sunny and cheerful, and so was this one.

Being June, there was still enough light when I got back to Langport for a trip to the wood. I did want to have a go at cutting back the ebullient growth from the rootstock of two grafted apples, before eagle-eyed visitors remarked upon it the next day. As soon as I assessed the job realistically, it was obvious it would take too long.

Instead I just wandered round and was rewarded, up above the hazels, by becoming aware of a gentle, bumbling sort of movement. Something bigger, quicker, shot through the undergrowth but the gentle bumblers, about the size of stout cats, took their time, emerging fleetingly into the dim light . . . badger cubs. Nothing anyone can say about Bovine TB, or overpopulation, or badgers eating hedgehogs, or of their not being respectable characters as in *Wind in the Willows*, can detract from the joy of seeing young badgers.

I have long known that there are badgers living in a sett just above the Disputed Territory, but hardly ever seen them. They are, in the RSPCA's alluring words, 'nocturnal and crepuscular'. Also discreet, as befits a species with 'a prolonged history of persecution'. The decline in gamekeeping has helped them, and the 'Protection of Badgers Act, 1997', but their favourite food, earthworms, is getting harder to find, and so is tranquil woodland for the maintenance of their ancestral setts. Seeing them so unexpectedly that June evening was like a gift, a good omen, or so I chose to think, for the 'Ebenezer' event.

Back at the cottage, I used the very last of the light to pick roses to decorate the Seed Factory for the talk the following day. There was an ulterior motive, in that *Albéric Barbier* is a phenomenal grower. Though it is pleasing to sit surrounded by roses, to sit with them scratching you is not, and bucketfuls of their yellow buds and white flowers needed to go.

It was in a collection of Vita Sackville-West's garden journalism that I first read of this rose. She says it is good for growing up old trees. She did not mention that an old apple tree may not like it, but it now occurs to me that letting *Albéric Barbier* loose upon one, as I did in the London garden, is akin to planting brambles underneath.

I knew, and had notes of what I wanted to say at the 'Ebenezer' talk, but was also aware that it was unlikely it would come out as planned. This is because of preferring, as a listener, the spontaneous to the tightly read sort of talk, and also of a sensation I have, as a performer, of this not really being me. A more extrovert double seems to take to the stage, but then departs the moment the show is over, along with the memory of what it said.

There was plenty of support for me, starting at the back in the form of a reassuring man with a computer, who demonstrated the use of a presentation clicker. There was the kindness of several friends wishing me well and, on stage, the stuffed dog, the roses, the grand piano. Tony Anderson, the organiser, said not to worry if some of the audience nodded off, although this time it might not happen because they were offering tea, not alcohol, in view of the early start and planned walk.

As the room filled up I sequestered myself in a pantry-like closet, the nearest thing to a green room in the Seed Factory. Into it, Lucy Willes, a fellow former student of the Ruskin School of Art, ushered John Newberry, our one-time tutor. In the fifty years since I had last seen him he had changed very little, still tall, kindly, slightly shy, but there was no falling upon each other like old friends, as that is not what we were. I had not expected him to remember me, but after a while he ventured, 'Did you have long hair?' It had been the 1960s so that was a safe bet, but yes, I did. Our brief meeting was richer in goodwill than communication, but when I met him again not long afterwards it emerged that he had woken on the morning of the talk hardly able to hear, so to have come at all was noble.

The hall had filled up. Tony said we would start promptly, and we did. What I had wanted to say was two-fold, an illustrated re-telling of how I had started planting trees for the love of it, and in hopes of leaving something good behind, but with the addition that I now disowned the calm optimism for the future expressed at the end of A Wood of One's Own. Instead, I was seeking to know more of how climate change, international trade, industrial agriculture and building development are threatening my speck of the natural world.

It is unlikely that many in the audience were discomfited by anything I did say; about the vanishing rabbits, for instance, there was no stir. But they did not appear to be asleep, at least not in the front rows. They were certainly awake when a man got up and introduced himself as a member of Extinction Rebellion. The name brought forth a mixture of growls and approving murmurs before he exhorted us to plant thousands of trees in Aller.

At first I was sympathetic but then that waned when it seemed that he was not interested in where the trees might grow. That appeared to be an irrelevant detail. I am much in favour of the rising popularity of tree-planting, but do wish it would extend to a focus on practicalities; what sorts of trees, where, and who will look after them.

Some trees planted in this (short-lived?) enthusiasm will doubtless survive by default. I often pass a triangle of ground on the way out of London, squeezed between major roads and a separate, unpromising site allocated to a community of Travellers. Year after year, good, decent-sized young trees would be planted on this triangle and, year after year, left unwatered till most of them died in their first summer. One early survivor put out side shoots the following year, making a brave if unbalanced growth. Its resilience has been followed by others so that now, years, wasted money and some rainy summers later, there is a raggedy group of young trees. If only they had been watered in their first year . . .

The conventional answer to this grumbling is that young trees are cheap while the labour involved in watering is expensive, and that the story I have just told proves that persistent planting works. Well, maybe. Politicians competing for votes were briefly keen on trees, conjuring thousands and millions of them into forests full of instant wildlife. (Oliver Rackham says it takes hundreds of years for a wood to gather itself and its web of life together.) Meanwhile, all saplings have to come from somewhere. To waste them through lack of care, having perhaps risked importing yet more diseases in the process, would take the shine off what is called a 'win—win' enterprise.

By the end of the talk, just as we had hoped, a damp afternoon had given way to a fine evening, so the tour of the wood was on. Tony had taken trouble over planning the movement of the audience; there was to be a shuttle service in a trio of old Land Rovers. To be there to welcome people, I was supposed to be in the first one. We had entertained thoughts of an orderly tour. Detained by conversation, however, I was among the last to leave the Seed Factory.

Until then I had had no idea what fun the ride would be, but roaring through the soft evening light in a very old Land Rover, all fresh air and flapping ties, stands out as a favourite part of the whole event. By that time, many visitors had already taken off in directions of their own. A young girl found a tiger moth, I went with some people along the boundary walk, discouraged one from questing into the Disputed Territories, agreed with another that the rootstock was indeed taking over a grafted apple, and heard from a third that she was a cello teacher. I know a lot more was said to me, but apart from a few snatches of conversation, some comical, recall nothing until Tony was getting people into the Land Rovers again. Soon the wood was quiet and, back at the Seed Factory, he was pleased with how everything had gone. I was just trying to readjust, now that my extrovert double had left.

All along my fear had been that the visitors would be disappointed. If so, they were too polite to say so. I did hear afterwards from some who had enjoyed themselves, been surprised by how much of the ground was open, or how it sloped, and from several who understood why I love the place.

Later on the same evening, when able to compare notes with my brother and sister-in-law on their party and the wood event, we agreed on being pleased to have done them and even more pleased that they were over, specially without any dramas from steep steps or rabbit holes.

∽

There is nothing like a deadline for getting things done. Even though not everything was done before the visitors came to the wood, I did still bask afterwards in the mown track and paths, the weeded beds around the Rollalong, the temporary absence of overhanging brambles. It was also surprising how much better it felt to have removed some ugly uprooted tree stumps from the all too prominent position they had, through a misunderstanding, been occupying.

Not that moving them had been easy, dryer and lighter though they were after their two years in the sun. It had involved placing the wheelbarrow in kneeling elephant position, pushing, shoving, then what I cared to imagine were serene thoughts about balance, before some blundering over rough ground. The heaviest stump never made it before toppling out, but in a less eye-catching place.

Only after this sequence did I realise how uncomfortable it had been to see those dry, dark, sad-looking root stumps. It was as though there were something inherently wrong in roots being in that state. While we are used to how some roots, like those of beech trees, show their entwined, beautiful sophistication in banks, they are then alive. To see them dead and sticking up brings altogether different associations; of battlefields, storms, fires, deforestation.

Tree roots, as we are becoming more and more aware, have their own busy underground life of communication and reciprocity, enabled by a magical-sounding web of mycorrhizal fungal species. The 'wood wide web' is a recent discovery, made by researchers in the temperate rainforests of western North America, and only described in the journal, *Nature*, as lately as 1997.

Almost without exception, the research upon which Peter Wohlleben has drawn for his book, *The Hidden Life of Trees*, dates from this century, so it is a very live topic. Wohlleben has given it a friendly face, offering a readable synthesis from scientific papers and making trees sound almost human; at least the more co-operative aspects of being human.

Later in the year but early in the morning, I had the pleasure of meeting him, briefly, in London. Although far from the forest he manages in Germany and just off the plane, he arrived looking fresh and awake. And, as I was pleased to see, rather like a tree . . . tall, handsome, dressed in a three-piece suit of brown tweed, with a neat version of the Green Man's beard. Maybe when you work empathetically among trees for a long time, categories start to blur . . .

∾

Still early in June, the *rugosa* roses near the Rollalong were coming into bud and Turkish irises that I once rescued from a building site were about to open. But I left before seeing either of these in flower, which is the drawback to living in two places.

A fortnight later, after some rain, the grass and everything else had rocketed. At first I thought I could hear the cuckoo, but no. Most summers I do hear that unforgettable call, so warm, so promising, from somewhere among the reeds on the moor. And they were here this summer, as people living nearby later told me. Cuckoos coming to Britain are in such drastic decline that it is good to know that they have not yet failed to arrive. Unless, that is, you are a reed warbler, or a meadow pipit, or a dunnock, and get tricked into raising one cuckoo instead of a clutch of your own eggs.

To my feelings, there is something very unsettling about parasitism, as though brilliant mimicry, or the other ways parasites have evolved to take advantage, are just not fair. But nature, whether imagined as a Mother or not, is capable of all sorts of grotesquerie, for instance, what a nematode does to the insides of a slug. I have no wish to rediscover the video which showed me this process, but here is a description from the RHS journal . . . 'the infective juvenile nematodes gain entry to hosts through such natural openings as mouth, anus or breathing pores. Once inside, they release a toxic bacterium which kills the host in 24–48 hours.' The video images, which fortunately did not play for 48 hours, were worse than the words. Two days is a long time for a slug to be deliquescing from the inside. Reed warbler chicks being pushed over the rim of their own nest by the cuckoo chick is mild in comparison.

No cuckoos that June morning, and no rooks either, it seemed. They, having taken the trouble to raise their own chicks high up in the ash trees, may by this time have been free to leave the wood by day, perhaps to demonstrate to their offspring the skills involved in making a rook living. Probing about in the open ground or grass for insects, grubs, worms or seeds would make up most of the curriculum. Which, according to the RSPB book, should be helpful to farmers 'as many of the insects they eat are harmful to crops'.

Farmers, however, have not generally seen it that way. From the old practice of paying young children a pittance to throw stones at them all day to the more recent one of having a man in combat gear with a gun, it has seemed worthwhile to 'persecute' them, as the book puts it. I still find a few shotgun cartridges in the wood, although not so many as there used to be. With scarcely a rabbit left, pigeons may be the targets, but rooks are more likely. That morning all I heard was a jackdaw sounding plaintive, some drumming from the green woodpecker and a lot of singing.

Many more of the mauve and buff flowers of the unfairly named stinking iris had opened since early June. They are quite at home in shade, unlike the yellow flags. Compared with grander irises they may be modest, but they are just as elegant in form, and more subtle in colour. The white and gold Turkish iris from the London building site was still just in flower, looking better in its green, rough surroundings than it had in Barnsbury.

Further up on the chalkier soil, the pyramidal orchids were popping up. I remember roughly where to expect them, but having recently been to a talk about British wild orchids I now know that they are sensitive about the right conditions, sometimes spending whole seasons underground, not dead, just waiting. Why, in the same area, some and not others come up, is beyond me to say. The wood is always full of such mysteries as far as I am concerned, with new ones ready to appear at any moment. It feels as though you could spend years examining what is going on inside a window box, never mind in four acres of land packed with life, visible and invisible.

❧

The Somerset Levels are interesting and arresting throughout the year, but on midsummer evenings, they can be so softly, so surreptitiously beautiful that . . . that what? Well, the heart-stopping, breathtaking clichés are actually right and the best thing is to stop and look. It was like that on my way back from a visit a few miles away, along a little-used, narrow road running between ditches and willows, pastureland on either side with open views to the west, wooded escarpment to the east.

The road being quiet, some drivers like to accelerate along the straight stretches. I am not such a romantic as to imagine that everyone wants to dawdle to enjoy the light, so had turned off into a gateway. Cattle were clustered in a small group under a willow, not appearing to be doing much more than flicking a fly away with a tail, and keeping each other company. They were of various colours and markings, black and white, fawn, dark red, grey. It would be untrue to claim they looked timeless, with the yellow plastic tags in their ears, but they did look perfectly at ease in their surroundings.

Such scenes were so common for so long that it would hardly seem worth mentioning a few cows by a gate, except that they are now nothing like so common, and getting rarer. As the smaller farms have been sold up and the bigger ones keep cattle indoors, and we worry about the methane they produce, and even read of cell-based meat being grown in a 'bioreactor', it is no wonder that I looked upon those sunset beasts with affection, and a sense of approaching loss.

Signposts are another vanishing commodity. There are turnings along that idyllic road where I am always in doubt, because some just lead to farms, but there is one that looks as though that is all it will do until it snakes past, going on to hug the bottom of the escarpment.

That wooded lane has a surprise along it; a near vertical rose garden which, as it seems to me with my hazy navigational skills, is not always there. It was in tune with the midsummer evening to find that this time, the rose garden *was* there. The roses are very tall, extensive and old-looking, growing on either side of a shadowy house. The place looks too dark for roses but there they are, or sometimes are.

Rose Garden in the woods

From the Summer Solstice to the Autumnal Equinox

Cows in the shade
on a hot day in July

Thistles cut in May come again next day,
Thistles cut in June come up again soon,
Cut them in July, they'll be sure to die.

Thistles in flower
r going to seed 10/8/20

H IGHER PLOT FARM, THE HOME OF Mr and Mrs Scriven, was the main attraction of the auction at which I bought their separate holding, Sugg's and Long Hill Orchards. A couple took on the small but heroically unmodernised farmhouse and, little by little, did it up themselves. Their idea had always been to improve, then sell it. But when it was at last for sale I asked how they could bear to leave all their work and that astonishing view.

To my surprise they blamed the road. It had got so much busier, they said, since the supermarket opened in Langport and the abattoir was enlarged. Which I suppose is true, although the road had always seemed noisy to me, and was the reason I had hesitated about buying the wood in the first place. Sound carries for miles in a flat landscape. In this case it is not the constant growl of a major road in the distance. Instead, when the traffic is light it is just the gradual crescendo and diminuendo of sound from a single car or motorbike, lasting so long that there is no moment of quiet before the next one starts.

In a dreamy moment in a half-remembered children's story, someone is sitting on a grassy bank on a warm evening, listening to the sound of a two-stroke engine as it comes and goes, drifting around the countryside. Despite the driver of the two-stroke being, I think, a wolf, the atmosphere is so benign and peaceful that I have occasionally tried to turn motorbike sounds heard from the wood into something like it . . . not an easy thing to do.

Anyway, Higher Plot Farm was sold and its new owners also arrived with a scheme, this time to do with the land. They had already had tests done on the soil to find that it was suitable for vines, and the hillside gets plenty of sun. They now have a successful vineyard.

When the house was still uninhabitable I had sometimes walked through the field that is now the vineyard, in order to avoid a couple of dangerous bends in the road. To my untutored eye, the sward looked interesting, with a variety of herbage. I mentioned this to Guy of the incipient vineyard, in case it might be an old hay meadow he was about to dig up. He took this calmly, saying that he thought it unlikely, that no one else had made such claims for it. And they would be leaving the turf around the edges and between the rows of vines.

The lament for vanishing hay meadows, with their insect-friendly herbs and flowers, lay behind my wondering about that grass. The charity Plantlife says that, compared with 1900, we only have about 1 per cent of former hay meadows left. This is because they were part of the small-scale mixed farming that has given way to intensive methods of food production.

The charity works to conserve what remains, to promote the extension of the wildflower field margins that arable farmers are meant to be sowing, and to encourage local authorities to be sensitive with the mowing of roadside verges. If you pass a verge with a strip near the road shorn so that we can see the corners, but behind that a strip with the mixed herbage growing tall, that suggests the local authority has been listening.

On a smaller scale, the planting of lawn-sized wildflower meadows was given a boost by the success of the Olympic Park (now Queen Elizabeth Park) in 2012. But these lawns are tricky. The 'wildflower mix' may start off well enough, a cheery assembly of, for instance, poppies, cornflowers, buttercups, oxeye daisies, red campion, white campion, yarrow, ribwort plantain, salad burnet and self-heal, but it can dwindle to only one or two of those by the next summer.

As with woods, it is not just a matter of dropping in a few seeds and expecting a whole community of plants and creatures to spring up, as fine and interrelated as the meadows and woods that have taken centuries to mature. However, when Guy of the vineyard and I met for coffee in late June, we were not concerned with sward but with comparing notes about our boundaries with the woodland further up, and whether we should be worried about fresh rumours of future redevelopment.

It is hard to stay worried when you are having a friendly talk in a friendly coffee shop. The serious part of our conversation soon trailed off into something more enjoyable . . . Guy had seen a polecat, just above his land. At least he had seen something, and reference to YouTube told him that it was a polecat.

Since my knowledge of polecats had not extended beyond imagining some sort of cat, I later enjoyed becoming acquainted with the images YouTube has to offer of a greyish, smallish mammal, related to stoats, weasels, ferrets and even badgers, with an appealing black and white face and sharp teeth. To judge from the videos, shot in the ghostly light of night cameras, polecats eat birds.

One of the videos starts off with a hen taking a misty dawn look about her untroubled surroundings. But then the music

turned ominous and I switched off. I have an extra soft spot for
hens. It was, I gathered, for its attacks on poultry that we brought
the polecat near to extinction in this country. But its numbers
have been on the increase since the 1950s and now it is as often
killed on the road as by farmers or gamekeepers.

A few days before my conversation with Guy, I had caught
the most glancing sight of something fleet and grey in the undergrowth edging the top orchard. A stoat, I thought, and was not
inclined to reimagine it as a polecat because the colour looked
wrong. To reimagine it as another of its relatives, the pine marten,
would have been promising, because pine martens hunt grey
squirrels, but I still think it was a stoat. Guy also said that he had
heard a nightingale (of which I was so jealous I chose to doubt
him) and that owls are often around but not rabbits. Rabbits are
as rare as hens' teeth.

In July, away I fly

In a favourite passage of one of my favourite novels, *Austerlitz*,
W. G. Sebald evokes a time spent 'looking into the mysterious
world of moths'. On a moonless summer night, Great-Uncle
Alphonso has taken Gerald and his school friend, Austerlitz, up
the hillside behind the house in North Wales, equipped with an
incandescent lamp. It is the 1950s, so there are plenty of moths.
As soon as the lamp is lit, the moths start gathering round it.
Gerald and Austerlitz are amazed by the strangeness and variety
of these silent creatures, appearing as though from nowhere.

Deftly, Sebald conjures the moths, the place, the atmosphere of this evanescent scene.

It follows another passage, of Great-Uncle Alphonso recalling the diversity of life in the Cornish rockpools of his own childhood which, already by the mid-twentieth century, were 'glories . . . almost entirely destroyed by our passion for collecting and by other imponderable disturbances and disruptions'. *Austerlitz* was published in 2001, the year Sebald died. Only now, looking into the book in search of those moths, do I pause to notice the reference to imponderable disturbances and disruptions, and wonder about them. Presumably he meant climate change, although it is hard to imagine him employing such a blunt term.

An activity that sounds magical in fiction may not be so in real life, but it was certainly this passage that had made me long for a night-time moth outing in the wood. For a while I had heard of a local Moth Man but it was not until early July that I went to look for him. The directions had a sufficient degree of vagueness to lend the sense of a quest.

The evening sun was still warm when a choice of three front gardens presented itself. Big bushes of lavender filled one, the second had a Union Jack, the third, a mixture of low-growing plants. Insects love lavender so that was the door I picked, wrongly, as it turned out. But the woman of the lavender knew straight away who I wanted and sent me past the Union Jack to the third door, at which Anne Bebbington and an excitable spaniel gave me a lively welcome.

I was a stranger but, so it emerged, John Bebbington had been tipped off by another member of the moth network about my interest, so was not surprised. By contrast, I was surprised, and chuffed at this access to a recherché circle. The dog was also surprised and needed calming. Anne offered me a biscuit to give to her, so then we would be friends. I gave the spaniel the biscuit . . . it seemed our friendship was not yet firm, so John ushered me into the front room and shut the door.

Anne, John soon told me, is a botanist and botanical artist. They met years ago while in competition for the same job, then another job was made available. They have been together ever since, raising a family, collaborating on projects, writing, drawing, photographing, travelling, giving joint lectures, leading tours. However easy it is to exaggerate the blessings of others, this story did sound enviable.

Our subject, however, was moths. John reports a shocking loss of them during the twenty years he and Anne have lived in Langport. It is the same period that I have known the area, so I recognised what he was describing when he talked about the old Kelway's Nurseries site. Kelway's, now a shadow of their pre-war, let alone Victorian selves, have moved from their original site. They used to own plenty of land in Langport and Huish Episcopi, handsome buildings and a number of fine trees, like redwoods, planted soon after they were introduced.

The tall stone buildings, for activities such as seed drying, processing, packing, were being renovated for other purposes when I first knew them but the big, partly walled gardens behind were a wilderness of forgotten plants, decrepit greenhouses, brambles, weeds and, so John was telling me, moths. His cottage is near enough for the moths to fly to his back garden of a summer night, get trapped, identified and then released. There were often well over a hundred species visiting in one night.

That mothy multitude is now gone, the wild gardens having been replaced by houses, pavements, street lamps, cul-de-sacs with names like Peony and Iris, in memory of the flowers for which Kelway's Nurseries were internationally famous. There is no Moth Way, but then only a few specialists would have known or cared about them.

I used to enjoy wandering around that derelict site, taking a few cuttings or collecting seed. If I noticed the insects it was only in passing, my main memory is of delicious blackberries. The wood offers blackberries but these were better. One hot August afternoon a friend and I gathered more than we could possibly want, in no time at all. My friend was Swedish, the daughter and sister of nurserymen, and I dimly sensed then that there was something poignant for her in that place and activity. Like most Northern Europeans, Swedes are great berry-pickers. I know that she remembered that moment afterwards, but it is too late now to probe the layers of what made it special for her.

John remarked that another building development is threatened on the other side of the road. Despite being also a good site for moths, he said that no amount of objection from him or others of like mind could save it. I asked why not; isn't nature conservation supposed to be further up the agenda by now? The answer was, these are only common moths, so unworthy of concern.

But how common is common? The theory of 'shifting baseline syndrome' often crops up in books about the current plight of nature. It describes how we remember the state of things, such as the abundance of moths, in our childhood. It is easy to mistake this memory for how things always were, so childhood memory becomes the baseline from which to measure further change.

Post-war, many wildflowers, insects, birds, etc., were more numerous than they are now. I did indeed assume that that was how things were. But that childish understanding overlooks the fact that nature, in the geological era we inhabit, had already been threatened for centuries, if not millennia. The botanist and Quaker, William Bartram, wrote ecstatically of the lush world around him on his travels in the wilds of what would become the South Eastern states of the USA. Even then, between 1773 and

1778, he was sorrowfully aware of the damage that plantation and development were bringing to the natural surroundings, and to the native peoples of them.

Going further back in time to more dramatic shifts in the baseline, George Monbiot writes staggeringly, in *Feral*, of the great beasts, or megafauna, that once flourished upon this planet. But, although the Mendip caves did shelter the bones of mammoths, I will not linger among beavers the size of black bears, or ground sloths with the weight of elephants, except to mention Monbiot's striking observation, that it was probably humans who got rid of them by hunting, rather than that they died from the effects of natural disaster. Whether we should mourn these beasts, or rejoice that they are no longer here to scare us, is hard to know.

So, thanks to these shifting baselines, a common moth can now be becoming rare compared with a few decades ago, without anyone in the planning department seeming to notice. When I note down the presence of a single rabbit, or tortoiseshell butterfly, I know how impoverished these sightings are, but if I were a child now, I might grow up thinking that rabbits and butterflies are meant to come in ones.

John and I were discussing the possibility of his carrying out a moth survey at the wood when he asked me what flowers are around. Why such a simple question should cause my mind to empty I cannot say, but it took some scrabbling to come up with a measly list of grasses, moon daisies, knapweed, thistles. I even forgot nettles and brambles, but luckily John did not seem to be put off. July would be better for moths than August, he said, although prior commitments might get in the way.

I was to acquire ultraviolet proof glasses because the moth-attracting lamplight can cause retinal slippage; not a detail that seems to have bothered Great-Uncle Alphonso. The website of the supplier John recommended revealed how specialist a world

Picture Wing Flies on
Burdock flowers
august

I was approaching, one in which an owl pellet dissection kit is listed under Gift Ideas, and a malaise trap or beating tray need no explanation. I felt some misgiving as I read on. If insects are in trouble, the idea of trapping, perhaps killing them does not sound all that good.

But still, I went ahead with ordering the glasses and was pleased when John said he would go for a daylight reconnaissance. Even more pleasing was the email in which he said that he had spent an afternoon in the wood and found much to interest him, although not the clearwing moths he had been hoping might be there. He did, however, see plenty of other things, flies, moths, crickets, butterflies, enough to make him think an evening's light-trapping could work well . . . 'there are sheltered areas if it is windy and, if it is a still night, the open area below the Buddleia bushes could provide an interesting catch'. A still, warm, cloudy night would be perfect, he said, and a rainy, windy one would be no good at all.

John sent five photos taken on that initial visit. Because he is a serious photographer I asked him which came first, the insects or the photography. It was the insects, he said, he had been interested in them since he was three, the photography came later, to service that interest. The images of the Peacock, Gatekeeper and Brown Argus butterflies were a pleasure to see, but the Burdock Picture-wing Flies were a complete novelty to me.

In John's photo, which shows things a touch larger than life, the flies are clambering around the burdock flowers and their spiky surroundings, the encirclement that will mature into a burr. The magnification shows that every hook that may attach itself to passing fur, cuff, scarf or sock, the brilliant system of seed dispersal that drives me mad later in the year, is already forming. But here the plant was more youthful, innocently providing nectar and, as I was later to see, a sleeping place.

From the Summer Solstice to the Autumnal Equinox

The flies, when I was able to see them in person, were enchanting; dainty, yellowish of body, their wings a faintly glistening mixture of transparent and opaque. The brown wing patterns did not, to me, amount to pictures, but it is often a puzzle to see what the coiners of common names could see. The flies appeared to be treating the burdock flowers as an obstacle course. At 4 o'clock on a hot afternoon they were very active, doing skittish-looking wing and leg stretches, but when I went back three hours later they were slowing up. Burdock flowers swell outwards above their stems, like thistles. It was to the shelter underneath that bulge, where they rested upside down, that the flies were retiring.

To be in the wood that afternoon, with plenty of shade, felt wonderful after hot London. For weeks the weather had been warm and dry so the grass had not grown much and the mown paths were still there, not trim, but easy to walk along. I carried cans of rainwater to the newly planted trees. They were alive and well, all but a forgotten seedling mountain ash, still in its pot.

Luckily mountain ash, or rowan, is a tough native tree and this one recovered after a few days of watering. It had originally seeded itself in a scrape of the sort of soil that seems to fall from the sky, on the decaying roof of the henhouse in London. Before starting on life in two places, we used to keep bantams, from my cousin's farm, at the bottom of the garden. They did well, and were approaching the age of fourteen, but then the fox moved in. Despite the dug-in wire defences, it turned out to be only a matter of time . . .

Of the two wych elm props put in to support the Hermit's Apple, one had vanished into the undergrowth but the other was now being leant upon. The tendency of the whole ensemble is undoubtedly downwards, but what remains of the tree was decked in bright, ripening fruit.

Nearby, some of the young grafted trees were also looking promising, fruit-wise, if not in their stance. Something, a deer I guess, had been stripping one of their branches of leaves. The ground was too hard to get a stake in but a branched piece of buddleia wood slotted into one of the dry fissures. The apple bough, with its remaining leaves and half-formed fruit, allowed itself to be draped over the buddleia twigs in a pleasing, albeit temporary fashion.

It was quiet up there, not much birdsong, no rooks.

෴

Spurred on by paintings of trees in two recent exhibitions, of work by Bonnard and Van Gogh, I had decided to see if any of my tubes of oil paint, untouched for decades, were still useable. The majority did feel soft, so I brought them to Somerset, in case I, too, could paint trees. To return to any activity after so long has its alarms, but to return to painting, which properly requires a lifetime's dedication, felt downright cheeky. On that first July evening I was not rushing into anything. I sat near the Rollalong with a sketchbook, facing an unspectacular view of the middle orchard.

Wild plums and elders made a dark frame. Ahead was a series of receding bands of colour, the greens of nettles and grass, a thin strip of mauve thistle flowers, then the pale gold of long grass with reddish-brown tops, finally a curtain of mid- and dark-green thicket.

What struck me was nothing to do with the picturesque; it was that, contrary to my feeling that the rams had not eaten much, they had in fact made a big difference to the grass. Where they had been able to reach, it was fresh green, where they had not, the pale gold began, a distinction I had not appreciated when walking around. Just settling down to draw, well or badly, is its own reward in terms of stilling the mind.

From the Summer Solstice to the Autumnal Equinox

This visit was during a period when successive news bulletins of record-breaking temperatures seemed to be placing the sun in its own Personal Best sort of competition. The day after I arrived was one such. By late afternoon when I returned to the wood, the barley had been cut in the big field. It had looked the wrong sort of colour the day before, dirty brown/grey rather than golden, so to leave it any longer might have been the death of it. The lines of stubble curved round the corner of the wood, making a bold swirl, and a rabbit dashed across it, looking very much alive.

When I left, after a bit more wrong-time-of-year branch propping, the lines of barley stubble were lighted-up ochre, the sky of palest blue was shading to opal, with long feathers of grey and peach, the Quantocks were velvety in the distance. The hottest day was leaving the countryside looking as serene as anyone could wish.

It is an irony of our changing climate that, for Northern Europeans not yet very seriously afflicted by fire, hot summer days are a treat. That the heat bakes the land so that rain, when it comes, runs off and floods, is not likely to worry families on the beach.

The four grandchildren of my late brother, Peter, with their attendant parents, were due to visit the wood within the next few days. With an age range of nought to seven, I had been wondering how this would all work out, thinking of nettles and other hazards. But looking at the barley stubble reminded me of the summer holidays my brothers and I used to spend at our grandmother's house in West Somerset, how we loved joining in with the harvest, even with bare ankles shredded by stubble. No adults seemed to give a second thought to that. Although I can still conjure up how much the stubble-scratching hurt, it never put me off.

There were a lot of people working in the field then, and we were allowed to ride high up on the loaded carts. This was the 1950s; it must have been near the last gasp of small-scale arable fields, before the hedges were rooted up to allow in the combine harvesters. It was also before pesticides were widespread. One hot day we stood at the gateway to a field of cabbages, listening to the sound of countless caterpillars, munching. It was loud. By this stage it was becoming a field of stalks and there was that nasty smell of decaying cabbage . . . no wonder the coming age of pesticides seemed like a good thing.

These recollections persuaded me not to worry too much about the children's legs, that stings and scratches do not last as long as good memories. Both families were meant to come together but then rearrangements meant that they came separately, the older children first. We lit a fire to cook sausages and afterwards they dashed about, enjoying the freedom. The girl, a bold climber, was a short way up a hazel tree when the branch gave way and she tumbled down . . . for a few moments she cried pitifully and it was not clear what precisely was wrong, until she managed to whisper, 'nettle!' Within ten minutes she was back to her natural jauntiness.

The next day the second family arrived, indirectly from America. It was late afternoon. The baby was smiling in his mother's arms, the girl shy, until she was sitting at the table, tossing off bright abstract watercolours. To universal acclaim, all available surfaces were soon covered with damp and dripping paintings. She only stopped, regretfully, because we needed the table space. My nephew stayed for a while after supper, when his wife and children had departed to the Langport Arms Hotel. He is my brother's elder son, quiet, clever, still with the slight air of unworldliness he had as a child.

The following day we laid out a picnic near the Rollalong and relit the fire. The young painter was clear about where she wanted to sit. Her mother and baby brother had been awake since the small hours, so they were soon curled up to snooze on cushions in the lea of the wheelbarrow.

The rest of the day passed easily enough. It included a wood-land walk, during which my niece-in-law was touchingly eager to draw her daughter's attention to various wonders. But it seemed that most of the wonders the child was interested in were within her own imagination. Where, so I heard from her parents, she keeps company with sisters who happen to be Russian.

My brother had often helped me in the wood, even though he was ill. To my pleased surprise, my nephew said he wanted to help me there too. So the next morning, while the rest of the family were at soft-play, we set off with leather gloves, secateurs and loppers to begin a pincer movement through the brambles on either side of the second Arthur Rackham apple.

It was a companionable activity, which he said was more intellectual than he had expected. I had not thought of it in those terms, but it is true that a bramble has no intention of giving up easily, that you have to keep thinking about what you are doing.

Towards the end of the two hours I was alarmed suddenly to remember that, for reasons I have never understood, other old apple trees had come to grief once they were exposed to light and air. Les 'the orchard guru' is adamant that letting in more air around old apples can only do good, but on two separate occasions early on in my wood time, decrepit, still-living trees perished once bereft of the company of their brambles and elder scrub. Having since read about the 'wood wide web' gives me pause about that, although I never got as far as the roots of the brambles.

As is only too obvious from the work of loggers and from fires tearing through forests, the growth of centuries can be destroyed in minutes. Even the brambles my nephew and I had hand-cleared would take a season or two to re-establish. Not wishing to undermine our sense of shared achievement that morning, I kept quiet about all this as we packed up. At least our pincer movement was incomplete when we stopped, which may have been a blessing.

I had booked an afternoon trip on the river, but the boat owner was dubious about the weather. We texted each other several times, making very different claims for what we could see coming in the self-same sky. My brother and sister-in-law came from Bath, to see the family and join us for the boat trip. We were all up for it but it was clear that the boatman was not, so we changed the plan to a riverside walk. While the spirit of the party was not altogether positive at the beginning, it improved as we went along, and then there was tea.

As usual when I see his grandchildren, I wished that my late brother had lived long enough to know them.

❧

In August, away I must

❧

After a few days in London, carrying more watering cans, and a short stay in Purbeck with another configuration of the family, I was back in Somerset for my evening date with John Bebbington and, we hoped, the moths. He was to arrive at 9 p.m. I came earlier, with the UV protective glasses, warm clothes, torch and a modest array of things to eat. Modest because I was not sure of the protocol; does one treat moth-trapping like a picnic, or would that be frivolous?

There was a pinkish purple sunset in progress, two rabbits on the track, and the moon, so recently the slimmest of crescents, already beginning to look portly. It then seemed

Common Blue on Fleabane & Mint
Summer

to disappear, which I gather was the right thing for it to do, for a mothing evening. I lit candles in the Rollalong and got out two chairs, then, hoping to open the lower gate for John, went to meet him.

Too late, there was already a small red car nosing its way up the track. He had decided on his previous visit where to put the car and where to set up the tripod, considerations that began to make sense to me when I saw that a generator and big reel of cable were involved; more items that W. G. Sebald had not included. In fact there seemed to be any amount of stuff, so I fetched the wheelbarrow and loaded it with tripod, bag of books, clipboard, net, white cloth and some white netting.

John chained the generator, a nifty object about the size of a vacuum cleaner, to a fence post, explaining that generators (worth much more than vacuum cleaners) can get stolen from advertised Moth Evenings. This was an unadvertised Moth Evening, but thefts of equipment are so common in the countryside he was not taking any chances.

We laid cable between the generator and the chosen spot, near the flowering cherry. With the white cloth spread on the grass, John put the tripod above it, shifting its legs till he was satisfied it would not fall down and damage the bulb. Being somewhat lame, he made most of these arrangements one-handed, the other holding on to a stick. Once the tripod was safe he hung the lamp from the top, making sure it was not touching the netting. It looked like a big white pear. The white netting clothed the tripod, making three separate triangular bays open to the wide world, not like a trap at all. I kept quiet, waiting to see how this could work, but then John volunteered that it wasn't actually a trap. He did not go so far as to say what it was.

The daylight was going, it was nearly time to put on the protective glasses and switch on the lamp. John had suggested

I warn the neighbours about the brightness of the sudden light appearing where all is normally dark, but the wood hardly has any neighbours. I sat on a chair, clipboard on lap, with attached pencil and impressively long list of names of what we might see. John was too busy to sit down. As soon as the lamp was on and casting a bright white glow, he was ready to capture in transparent beakers anything he could not immediately recognise. For one who needed a stick while walking on rough ground, he turned out to be remarkably agile on his knees.

The moths were in no hurry. We waited for some minutes, hearing the owl hooting, the deer barking, squawks from a magpie. It was like having prepared a party . . . where are the guests? Little by little they came, but not, as people often say of the mothy clouds of the past, as a snowstorm. They seemed to become drugged by the light, attaching themselves to the white walls of the tripod or the cloth on the grass, unable to leave even though they were not enclosed.

John says it is not known for certain what draws moths to light . . . there are different theories. He mentioned one, dubiously, about the compound faceted shape of their eyes and the way bright lights upset their balance and ability to sort out what they are seeing, making them spiral about and get disoriented. It sounded like yet another way in which we humans mess up the lives of others.

We had a dung beetle arrive, some mayflies and smaller flies, a grasshopper, but mainly it was moths. A slim, pale little thing, *Chrysoteuchia culmella*, Garden Grass Veneer, became one of our most frequent fliers. During a lull, John opened up his bat detector, a device for registering the squeaks of bats which most adults cannot hear but are often audible to children and, as I now read, moths. Only a noisy grasshopper showed up on it. It is several summers since I have seen bats up there.

The Rosy Footman moth came next, more apricot than rose it looked, although that may have been the quality of the light. The Dingy Footman came too, looking elegant rather than dingy. John says there is a line down the side of the wing that made whoever named these moths think of a footman's livery. The namer was perhaps more used to seeing footmen than many of us are now. I guess the line looked like piping.

Our procedure was that John would call out either in Latin or English, and I would flap through the four pages, scanning the columns of unfamiliar names before putting in a tally mark. To be sure of the identity of some of the moths he would lunge forward with one of the transparent canisters, clap it over the creature as it clung to the white fabric, then quickly fasten the lid. The quarry would flit about inside, where it was easier to see.

Sometimes he needed to check in the book, because there have been so many changes, thanks to DNA testing and the advances in knowledge it has ushered in. The light from the lamp was easily bright enough for these activities. Then I would ask if we could let the moth go, which we usually could. Only a couple did he keep for further inspection at home in case they were something special, which, as he later told me, they were not.

As time went on more species turned up. Some keep later hours than others, apparently. There were no hoards, our best score of any of them was twelve, but we were kept busy. That top scorer was the Lesser Broad-bordered Yellow Underwing. From its name you might think that it was yellow on the underneath of its wings, but no, its yellow, bordered by black, is on the hindwings, often covered by the sober, patterned darkness of its forewings. Its larvae like primroses, cuckoo-pint, hawthorn, ivy, dock, willow, elm, nettle and violet, all of which the wood offers, so it would seem reasonable to regret that there were not more than twelve of them. I was also disappointed, given the havoc among plums wrought by maggots, that the Plum moth never came flying in. Only its relative appeared, the Chequered Fruit-tree Tortrix moth.

It was getting chilly. I went into the Rollalong to fetch a sweater and there were the biscuits, waiting, but they did not seem right for this intense, serious activity. John was not feeling cold and, no, he did not want a kneeler. Returning to the tally sheets, I asked whether we might not be counting some of the individuals twice, as they remained congregated on the white sheet. John acknowledged this possibility, but thought not.

Moths, as John's arrangement of our potential arrivals' names indicated, are divided into macro and micro species, although it does not follow that all macros are bigger, just that most of them are. The macro-moths took up three pages, with only one for the micro. Although there are more micro species in Britain, when John had later tabulated our numbers, most of them were indeed macros. None of them was really big. But Willow Beauty, of which we saw three, was certainly beautiful. It is a Quakerish sort of beauty, with the patterned wings as though embroidered into miniature loops and flourishes, using darker thread on light grey. Photographs of Willow Beauty spreading its wings on the bark of various trees, not just willow, illustrate how this fragmented effect is aiming not at beauty but disguise.

When I asked John if we would have had a better haul ten years ago his answer was an emphatic, 'Yes, what's happened in the last few years is really a disaster'. His explanation was habitat loss due to house building, and more intensive farming. I objected that no chemicals had been used on this patch for twenty years, and probably forever. But that argument fell straight to the ground, because chemicals come in on the wind.

On the other side of the road, fields that used to be pasture now produce arable crops, and, just a step beyond the wood is the big arable field, which is not run on organic principles.

Three years ago there was a crop of maize there instead of the usual wheat, followed in 2018 by flax. While I was hoping these deviations might herald a greater interest in crop rotation, Rob the organic farmer had a possible, more prosaic explanation.

Rob had heard that the field was badly infected by black grass, an enemy of arable farmers, which cannot be knocked back by the herbicides permissible for wheat production. Maize and flax are both grown for animal feed. He was not certain, but thought that what may have happened was the application of a stronger herbicide, capable of dealing with the black grass. Ah well, so much for my maintaining an island of purity.

In *Austerlitz*, the three moth watchers stay out on the hillside till daybreak. John, also, used to stay up with the moths all through the night, but not anymore. The two hours we had been out had gone very fast and it was time to pack up. Off went the lamp, out came the torch. The white cloth, which John shook vigorously to get the moths to depart, was damp with dew as I folded it up. I made a hash of rolling up the cable from along the path back to the generator. It splurged off its reel into irregular loops, which I, trying to hold the torch like a cinema usherette to light John's footsteps at the same time, chose to ignore. I would have chucked the whole muddle into the boot, to be sorted later. He, however, did not ignore it. We stopped, he struggling in the dark to unravel the loops and get them to lie down in their proper place. I was impressed, as I so often am, by the determination of others to keep things in order.

We parted at nearly midnight, with many good wishes. Back in the Rollalong it was warm, just from the burning of the candles. I ate a few biscuits, put away the chairs, locked up and departed, wishing all the moths well, especially those we had detained. I have heard it said that they only have about four nights to fly. On that basis, we had interfered with their activities for about a fourteenth of their flying lives. Which, from my lifespan so far would be about five years taken away. So, though I had loved and appreciated the evening, it made me a shade uneasy.

❧

John soon sent a list of our findings, followed by some photos from his collection. We had noted sixty-six moths, of thirty species. I was disappointed it was so few, because of the one hundred and fifty species he had recorded in his garden. Curious to see this insect-friendly haven, a few days later I visited John and Anne there. Though not a big space, it is divided into several smaller ones, with hedging and cordoned apple trees in between, a pond, moth traps, shed, greenhouse, pots of verbena standing on the steps of an old ladder, evening primroses, wisteria, roses, jasmine, clumps of longish grass and other plants I have forgotten. It felt like a close-stitched tapestry, a lot going on within a small compass.

It was not, though, so unlike other gardens that it was obvious to me what had attracted so many species. But then John explained, that richness was in the past, before the old Kelway's site had been developed into houses and lighted streets. Also, he said, it was quite cold the night we were out. Really? It was 10 p.m. before I felt chilly . . . 'it was cold for moths', was his gentle reply.

The photos John sent were from the resources he keeps for lectures. In real life, many of the moths had been so small and fluttery I had hardly seen them at all, but in the slight magnification of the pictures, what a series of wonders appeared . . . The Common Plume, for instance, is a creature I had sometimes noticed before without even knowing that it was a moth. Pale grey or fawn, more like a miniature light

Wonky
Angust

aircraft than a moth, it has long, impossibly delicate-looking wings, legs, feelers. It can unfurl its plumy wings, but I have usually seen them rolled up tight. We recorded one of them. Given that bindweed is listed among the plants its caterpillars eat, hundreds more would be welcome.

The Setaceous Hebrew Character looks textured, a sugar aquatint of a moth, with its markings a soft layering of dark brown, fawn and creamy white. 'Setaceous' means bristly, but either greater magnification is needed to show the bristles, or they are just what makes the moth look textured. Carl Linnaeus is credited with giving it its scientific name, *Xestia c-nigrum*, but it may have taken some scholarly clergyman, whose knowledge included Old Testament Hebrew as well as lepidoptery, to see a Hebrew character on its wings. Once you have been told what to look for you can see the character, picked out in dark brown on ivory, on the moth's neatly folded wing. Its caterpillars eat any number of plants, but chiefly nettle. We noted three of them, as moths.

The Rosy Footman, in John's photograph, is the colour of cooked crab, with a lazy, looping pattern doodled in soft brown across its wings, while the waves of the Small Waved Umber break with beauty and delicacy across the expanse of its outstretched wings and thorax. In charcoal, grey and fawn they follow each other, as though elves working overnight had helped Fair Isle women with their knitting, and produced something silkier, frailer, more dreamlike. The Dusky Thorn, in another picture, appears to be dressed in peachy taffeta, stepping out like a proper lady, or dandy, across the rough terrain of an old dry leaf.

All these, to me, were a revelation. Even if in an approximate, inattentive way, I had been brought up to be aware of the fascination of plants, birds, mammals and butterflies, moths were always marginal to this world of the Nature Table, the country walk, the 'O' level biology syllabus. They were the shadowy, lesser cousins of

'All Things Bright and Beautiful', that came out at night, were hard to see, secretive and, in an irrational way, scary.

Moths are, however, far from lesser cousins. In Britain, moth species hugely outnumber those of butterflies. As Brian Hargreaves and Michael Chinery say in their introduction to *The Collins Guide to Butterflies and Moths* (1981) 'it must be pointed out that the distinction between butterflies and moths is quite artificial and unimportant'. They further remark that few European languages other than English make a distinction between the two. Michael McCarthy, author of *The Moth Snowstorm*, backs this up with 'butterflies are just a branch . . . on the moth evolutionary tree'.

Moth numbers have been declining since the 1960s at so dramatic, and until recently, hidden a rate that it is almost unbearable to read about. I am a very late arrival at the Lepidopterists' Ball and greet the moths of the wood in a way that cannot help being tinged with sorrow.

On the printed copy of John's list of our sightings I have pencilled what, according to various authorities, their larvae eat. For instance, The Flame Shoulder eats dock and plantain, the Pretty Chalk Carpet, old man's beard, the Yellow Shell, chickweed, the Brimstone, hawthorn and blackthorn. And so on, through a list of plants (including bindweed, thistle roots, nettles, grasses, dandelions, bedstraw, ash, lichens, willow, violet, primrose, elm, cuckoo-pint, oak, plum) not all of which I was previously very keen about.

Marrying up the plants with the moths, though, how pleased I felt that the raggedy wood, with its mixture of open grass and boskage, has all along been providing a few of these astonishing creatures with what they need. It was the thought that perhaps more wild flowers and grasses would invite in more different moths that prompted me to contact Emorsgate Seeds, the purveyors of 'weeds'.

❧

The year was galloping along. I returned from a short stay in London to find that Laura had put in a group of ewes with their lambs. Compared with the rams in May, this all female party, at least as far as the adult sheep were concerned, was the model of decorum. They did not rush up as soon as I arrived but stayed among the thistledown in the middle orchard. Because of the height of the thistles it was hard to count them. Laura had said there were eleven, and one was called Wonky, because of her shoulder.

Among those I could see processing up and down the mown paths, eating the grass that least needed their attention, there was no obvious Wonky. A couple more drifted in and out of sight beyond the thistles, working the turfy bits near the fence. I could hardly blame them for going for green-and-springy as opposed to dry-and-thistly. Sometimes, big though they were, the lambs would turn to their mothers for a drink, shaking their long tails in excitement and pleasure. Or, if that sounds too anthropomorphic, in what looked entirely like excitement and pleasure.

It was not until gold light was pouring through the gaps in the hedgerow, illuminating some nettle flowers and apple leaves while others fell into dark-green shadow, that I came upon Wonky. She was unmistakeable, with her head held at a strange angle because of her shoulder. The light was making a halo behind shoulder, ear, brow and other ear, as though she were the patron saint of disabled sheep. She looked fine. Laura says that she should really have shot her, except that she is happy, and a character. And she has had a healthy lamb.

August, I had decided, was to be the moment for pursuing the idea that the water in the pond comes underground from the

Mendips, and is of remarkable purity. It is an idea that had stuck in my mind, more because I would like it to be true than because it is probable. Wells Museum seemed a good place to start.

The helpful volunteer who answered my call (the museum is run almost entirely by volunteers) said that there is a permanent display about Mendip caves, an interesting relief map showing river valleys, and any number of knowledgeable people among the volunteers, although she was not sure if anyone was an underground water specialist. I was to come on a Monday, when the curator, the only one not volunteering, would be most likely to be free.

On the following Monday, a different volunteer was in charge of the front desk, who seemed less inclined to think the curator might have a moment to spare. Perhaps at some point he might. Meanwhile, I was to look at the relief map and the display of the Mendip cave. Obediently, I found the relief map, a large and verdant creation on which a lot of skill and varnish must have been lavished long ago, when local railway lines ran every which way through North Somerset.

Partly because the map was displayed on a wall, making its three dimensional qualities feel vertiginous, partly because rivers seem to have been less important to its maker than railway lines, I did not feel I was gaining much insight from it, so proceeded to the staged interior of a Mendip cave. The rocky shaped enclosure was painted black. It was furnished with an assembly of pickaxes, boots, lamps, etc., with the sound of rushing water playing somewhere behind it. In terms of authentic atmosphere, it was reminiscent of pubs in the 1980s seeking to look Olde Worlde, with darkened beams portraying massy oaken strength, but flecks of white polystyrene showing through.

Before lassitude could overcome me, I left the cave and turned to a table where a volunteer sat, sorting through trays of shiny bits of black rock. He immediately took up my query, saying that the best thing would be to talk with another volunteer, an experienced caver. He led me to the back of the museum, through a garden to a prefab-type building, into which he disappeared.

A while later, out he came with the Experienced Caver. She was a bright-looking woman, and all the more impressive for appearing of an age not often associated with the demands of caving. Soon, however, she said that she was an ex-caver, not that she would not still like to be exploring caves, but that her hip would object. She listened to my proposition about underground water travelling from Mendip to the Aller Escarpment, the probability of which seemed to diminish with every word I spoke.

'Unlikely, I think,' was her succinct response, 'but let's look at some rock specimens.'

In an upper gallery was a display of rocks, including the Blue Lias and White Lias that underlies the wood, and various sorts of limestone. The pieces were about the size of thick dinner plates, big enough to give an idea of how they would have continued, had they not been broken. The reason for looking at them, as I gradually realised, was to understand how water moves through limestone, of which, roughly speaking, the Mendips are composed.

My guide was soon talking about 'uplift'. Taking the nearest piece of paper, she started to illustrate this concept. It is always fun to watch people drawing from imagination; when the pencil darts about and the lines set off to join points that you least expected would have anything to do with each other.

A running commentary ensued, as an incomprehensible succession of marks began to emerge on the page until, with the addition of a few extra lines, dots and arrows, suddenly there were the Mendips, looking like a row of cloches for bringing on salad crops. Another lower row indicated the Aller Escarpment with nothing to suggest any connection between them. The arrows heading straight down towards the ridge of Mendip were the rain, while the dots and diagonal lines are explained by a note, 'Carboniferous massive limestone with joints/cracks which allow water to move freely'.

The overall gist was that water is in a hurry to get to the sea, in this case the Bristol Channel, which lies to the west. Unless something in the underlying geology made it do so, it would not dawdle on its way by flowing south-west, being forced up again along the Aller Escarpment, from whence it would still have to reach the Bristol Channel via the River Parrett. My guide did not believe there was any such obstacle in the underlying geology. In further evidence, she stated that clay is impermeable, which made me think of my perpetually leaking pond and wish its clay bottom was listening.

The talk of obstacles led to the question of springs, that subject so wreathed in myth and surprise, at least to the non-geologist. At this point my kind helper said she had better get back to her task of putting old museum data into digital form. But I should meet her at the upcoming 'Ancient Springs of Wells Geo Walk' at the weekend. It was part of the 'Mendip Rocks!' festival and would be led by an excellent geologist. She put an X on the map of Wells where we were to meet, said to ignore any suggestion that the walk was fully booked, and bid me goodbye. Despite having heard nothing to support the Mendip spring water theory close to my heart, I went away in good spirits.

A few days later, at the appointed X, we met with the excellent geologist, and about twenty other enthusiasts. I was surprised by the site, a steep, scrambly bit of woodland above a road leading out of Wells. It was neither up on Mendip, where the rain finds its way underground, nor in Wells where the springs are, but in a former quarry grown in with pine, holm oak, ash, sycamore, hazel, hornbeam, yew, with occasional slabs of rock face exposed by the quarrying, a lot of roots and loose scree to trip on, and not a lot of space for twenty people to stand together.

The group was as varied, or essentially unvaried, as might be expected of such an event. It soon became clear that our amiable leader had to handle more people than would have been ideal, who brought widely different levels of knowledge. In other words, he was confronting what most state school teachers confront all the time, except that we were behaving ourselves. Or so it seemed, but then one senior Mendip Rocker complained of the background chatter, an intervention which, while not stilling all conversation, did cast a schoolroom chill upon the party.

Meanwhile, we looked at three 'quarried exposures'. With help (hence some of the background chatter) I tried to keep up. My impression was that it was all a hotchpotch, older limestone with calcite crystals cheek by jowl with younger (but not young) conglomerate pieces, bigger layered slabs of limestone infilled with calcite but also with a line of chert, not to be confused with calcite. Some of these were indicators of rainwater flowing through, or if not rain, hotter fluids, or cooler fluids.

Then we came to some red rock with veins of crystal, even a geode, but it was the yellowish vertical lines, like drips of paint, that our leader was most enthusiastic about. He thinks they are fossil roots, a suggestion that, as I understood it, had not been made before. The only mention of springs was at the beginning, when he remarked that they are probably 200 million years old. Not having properly attended to the title of the talk, I was not sure why we were looking at these ancient traces of flowing water when springs are still there, bubbling up, only a short distance away.

I had enjoyed this intriguing morning, but my new friend knew that it had left me little the wiser. She took the trouble to write several pages entitled 'Notes to Try to Explain where

Spring Water Comes From'. The third page of this lucid account is headed 'Area of Your Wood' and begins:

> *Looking at the British Geological Survey map on the Internet, and using the sketch map in your book, the rocks in your area are about 200 million years old. Basically you seem to have interbedded mudstone (impermeable) and limestones (permeable via joints perhaps, but not thick beds like the Carboniferous Limestone of Mendip). They will be nearer to horizontal than the Mendip limestone (which has been tilted to an angle of 30 degrees). This suggests to me that the water in your spring hasn't travelled very far. Caves are very unlikely and water movement will probably be via very small trickles in the rock.*

It had never occurred to me that there might be caves underneath the wood, so the regret with which I read that they were unlikely to exist was as quixotic as my whole pursuit of the fabled Mendip spring water. If this enquiry had been altogether rational, such a patient explanation would have been enough to settle the matter. But I was not quite ready, yet, to abandon hope.

It also made me smile to read of my sketch map in the same breath as the British Geological Survey for Bristol and Gloucester (which includes Mendip and the Somerset Levels). Turning to it, I enjoyed its talk of uplifts, depositions, unconformities, although geology asks a lot of the lay reader. Using everyday words like drift or fold, it describes the unimaginable; huge land masses on the move, whole bodies of rock forced to change shape. Reading through the survey, I was also drawn to phrases such as 'remains poorly understood', 'poorly known', 'not known'. Maybe there was some room yet for my travelling water . . . but really, it was only cussedness that kept me going.

A second opinion, arranged through a friend, cast new doubts about the water having come far: '*It is likely that the spring originates from one of the thin limestone bands within the Lias Clays and may perhaps be related to the fault shown on the map*'. So I looked at the map the friend mentioned, hoping to find the fault. The swirling outlines of the various areas of rock were filled in with textured autumnal colours, dull apricot for Keuper Marl, pinkish brown for Mainly Clay. It looked like 1960s furnishing fabrics. Among the layers and swirls I did, with difficulty, find the right area, but having read that a fault 'disrupts an orderly sequence', looked in vain for anything as exciting as that.

Another line of enquiry had entered my head. Local knowledge has it that there are springs all along Aller Hill. There is also a Somerset Lias quarry nearby. I wondered if the quarrymen might know something about springs and faults.

Do thy best, draw every day. Though it be little, yet will it be much . . .

*an approximation of advice given by an
Old Master painter to his apprentices*

Summer was passing and the glowing afternoon light was falling lower and lower across the grass. I have long remembered the sage advice of that Old Master painter, even though I cannot trace who he was, or claim to follow his rule. The forty-plus-year-old oil paints and new primed boards I had brought in a

Old Man's Beard
in flower & going to seed

August

moment of hope were still awaiting their time. When it came, I had to search around for the palette and other bits and pieces. There is any amount of stuff you need to remember to take, for painting outside.

As soon as I arrived at the wood and started trundling this collection up (the wheelbarrow was to be the stand for the table easel) the sheep made it plain that they did not intend to stand still and be models. The path leading to the cedars was my chosen spot. By the time I had easel, chair, stool for putting things on, palette, brushes, rags, white spirit and white board assembled, the late sun was spilling through gaps in the hedgerow and shining on ivy leaves attached to a leaning plum tree.

The grass of the path was green, beyond the reach of the mower it was tawny, mingled with brown seedy docks. There were bands of sunlight and shade. I looked with a mixture of excitement and trepidation. But this was premature, as it soon became clear that, though an old tube of paint may feel soft, that does not mean you can get the top to come off. Only three did come off.

The resulting 'restricted palette' consisted of Terre Verte, Light Red and Yellow Ochre. Not a bad selection, and anyone unshackled by the desire to represent the world in front of them might have been fine with it. But I wanted to catch that golden, not ochre light. At the Ruskin I did make an attempt at abstraction, at which a kindly tutor had said, 'why don't you try and put down what you see?' Why not? Because at that time, nearly a century's worth of progressive art practice had been throwing over the idea of just putting down what you see. I felt ashamed of being literal-minded and was trying to be otherwise. Nevertheless, his words were a comfort.

Anyway, it was good to be sitting there, making some marks, enjoying the cooing of the wood pigeons, wondering if I had once had a better range of brushes. The sheep were mainly in the middle orchard. But two, a mother and lamb, had got themselves stuck, as they seemed to experience it, in the first orchard with me blocking their way. I was not, actually, blocking their way. There was a lot of bleating communication between the two orchards.

If I looked round as the two played grandmother's footsteps to try to get past me, or worse, spoke encouraging words, they bolted back. So I acted unaware of what was happening out of the corner of my eye. At last, gallop gallop, they shot past and off to join the others. Much bleating, then all was calm again. I am not tempted to think *silly sheep*, because they doubtless had their reasons.

It was getting dark so I packed up the paints, a messy business, and felt it was time for a drink. My father once told me a story about holding off that desirable moment, just so you feel a bit more deserving. It was towards the end of the First World War and he and his Army companions were stuck in Damascus. They were bored, inclined towards the comforts of alcohol, and much afflicted by flies. They made it a rule that before anyone could have a drink, they had to kill twenty of their tormentors. I have often borne this in mind, although the tormentors are not usually flies. They might, for instance, be twenty items of washing-up, or pieces of household clutter to tidy away. On this occasion, I cut back twenty streamers of bramble.

There were a few owl hoots as I left. Looking from the track, the Quantocks were the softest mauve-grey, the sky a uniform hazy pink, but the Blackdown Hills had disappeared. The haze made it look as though the moor stretched to the horizon.

The following day I took pliers to the paint tube tops, most of which came off to reveal useable paint. They included some white, and cadmium yellow and orange, among more subdued colours. It was the same time of day when I returned to the painting place, but the light was less bright. The cadmium yellow and white made up for that. When it was getting too dusky to continue it seemed all wrong to waste any cadmium yellow (a tube of the same make currently costs £105) so I mixed it up with whatever-else-was-left into two or three different greens and sloshed them on wherever any of the white board was still showing. Putting things away in the Rollalong in candlelight, it looked as though the sloshed-on bits of the painting were better than the carefully considered ones.

Returning down the track in the twilight, it was good to see that the Blackdown Hills were back, but two bright lights moving on the moor were a less welcome sight. Poachers? And even more alarmingly, a four-wheel drive was storming around Philip's field, where most of Laura's sheep were, headlights on and with extra searchlights mounted on a high bar. Ever since Rob the organic farmer's sheep were stolen, never to return, rustling has felt a very present danger. I was afraid it was poachers driving the sheep into a corner, even if roaring round seemed an odd way to go about it.

Not feeling brave enough to intervene, I rang Philip. A short while later his wife called back, saying that all was well, it was Laura herself, topping the thistles and docks. Choosing to think that the bright lights on the moor might have an equally peaceable explanation, I calmed down.

∾

The first living creature I met on my next wood visit was not where it was supposed to be. Somehow a lamb had found its way inside the Rollalong enclosure where, did it but know, the zuggy pond was a danger to it. It was, however, looking relaxed, nibbling wild plum leaves. To leave the wooden gate wide open seemed as likely to invite more sheep in as to get the lamb to leave, but when I tried to persuade it through the half-open gate it just shot past, several times. If its mother was aware of the situation she was not hurrying over, but some bleating had started up.

I was afraid the lamb might be spreading the truth about how much greener the grass was on the Rollalong side of the fence. I fetched some rope, thinking to make a visual barrier to reduce the lamb's options, but by the time I was back, it was trotting out through the gate, waving its tail behind it. Though this sequence (longer than it may sound) did not suggest a future as a shepherd, I was pleased to have managed without texting Laura.

It was time to pack up the Rollalong. This used to involve diligent sweeping, mopping, and removal of anything a mouse might eat, including soap. Now there is so much extra stuff in there; scythe, new strimmer, wheelbarrow, easel, it is harder to do.

If only previous generations of fox or badger had not dug out the soil under the shed, the clutter could still be locked in there. They had been after the nesting rabbits and their excavations made the shed tilt so much it cannot be locked. I gave the Rollalong interior a lick and a promise, put the soap into a container and left. Now the rabbits are so few, repairing the shed has joined the list of good intentions.

The damsons, which I checked on the way out, were purple but still very hard. Making a date with my brother and sister-in-law for damson picking is a matter of guesswork; one year we left it till well into September and the too-ripe fruit was less good for jam.

As I left the light was stormy. It is often hard to park in Langport and on this occasion I went over the bridge before finding a space. It was darkish and raining as I walked back over the River Parrett. For a moment the low sun broke out and a tall, thin rainbow started growing up on both sides of the town,

Damson
Tree
Sept.

meeting faintly at the top. Across the moor towards Muchelney, the blowing leaves of whitebeam and the distant church tower were lit up, enough to show, ghostly, through the murk. Then the sun was gone, and with it, the whole picture.

September, blow soft, Till the fruit's in the loft

The damsons were softer, the ground harder, when I looked round the wood about ten days later. The sheep had been moved, but not far away. There were fallen apples and pears, a couple of recently planted trees were crying out for water. The thistles, however, were looking fine. I was carrying water for a young silver birch, eyes peeled for the autumn crocus. The hope had been that by now the autumn crocus would have multiplied into unmissability, instead of which its modest growth makes looking for it an annual excitement. There was no sign of it as yet, but there were unmissable signs of sheep.

This section of path is beyond where the sheep had been allowed, and anyway, Laura had moved them. Further along, bright in late sunlight, stood a single sheep, bleating. Having learnt from the last encounter that trying to drive it would be useless, I waited around, looking at this and that. The American Black Walnut sapling seemed all right, despite broken tap root and drought.

A while later, the path was empty. Soon I found a section of barbed wire with wisps of wool attached. The ground underneath slopes down from the ancient mounded boundary with Philip's orchard, giving some clearance for a young, venturesome sheep. As I was leaving, the damp, soft halo round the waxing moon looked in welcome agreement with the forecast of rain, except that we were planning to pick damsons the next day.

A damp grey morning, with every possibility of more rain, meant that we postponed the damson picking. I spoke instead on the phone with the Somerset Wildlife Trust warden for the area. I am sure there has been a falling off in numbers of insects, smaller birds and rabbits on my patch. But having no previous survey numbers against which to make a comparison, I wanted to know if he thought Aller Hill in general had been losing its wildlife. And in particular, what had been happening on the Trust's own reserve, Prospect Field.

The warden had known the area for nine years. Although it did not sound as though much surveying had been going on, he seemed quite sanguine about the state of local wildlife. However, they had tried planting thyme and marjoram in Prospect Field to support the Common Blue butterfly, without success. The rabbits, instead, had been the beneficiaries, although he did agree that there were hardly any rabbits now. He also remarked that there were no White Admiral butterflies, or nightingales. He thought that the polecat that Guy saw above the vineyard might have had some ferret in its family background.

Even without thyme or marjoram, there are often a few Common Blue butterflies fluttering round flowers like fleabane, thistle or mint on the shoulder of land below the Hermit's Apple. Common Blues do still seem to be quite common, fortunately. White Admirals, on the other hand, I had not seen, nor expected to see. The Woodland Trust website says that they like plenty of brambles and that their decline may be linked to habitat loss. Oh dear, I have caused the loss of a lot of brambles. But, as I guiltily exclaim to the absent Admirals, there are still a lot of them left, and honeysuckle for your caterpillars . . .

The day remained wet but, thinking the weather might do what it often does and clear up towards sunset, I went to the wood. The grass under the two damson trees is full of nettles, a hindrance to fruit pickers, so I was hoping to cut them back with the strimmer. It really was too wet. I crammed the stepladder and baskets into the Rollalong, ready for the next day.

As with so many creatures called 'Common', these baskets used to be so everyday that to notice them would have been like our noticing cardboard boxes. Things change, and now a sturdy, curvaceous basket with a looped handle, woven by hand from Somerset willow, is a thing to notice.

Alf Brewer made the baskets we were going to use. For a while his varied products, from 'tall narrow shoppers' to trugs and log baskets, were on sale at Pitney Farm Shop. For handmade items they were not expensive, and in surprising abundance. This was because, as Lizzie Walrond of the shop related, Alf could not stop making them. He was well past retirement age but the craft he had learned as a young man, before plastic knocked it sideways, held on to him still.

I, a frequent customer, was curious about the various sizes and shapes of basket designed for picking different sorts and quantities of fruit, about which I had read but not seen. Alf's handwritten labels would sometimes specify the basket's capacity; 2 Peck, 1 and a half Peck. Pecks are a measure of volume rather than weight, an unfamiliar concept, but I think it means that a 2 peck basket would hold the same 2 pecks, whether of apples or raspberries. From the look of these high-sided items, Alf must have been thinking of things hard enough to keep their shape, like apples, not squashable raspberries. It is because fruits vary so much in their squashability that there were so many different sorts of fruit basket.

It would have been interesting to talk of such things with an expert, but before the drawn-out process of me setting up a visit to meet Alf Brewer had come to anything, a hiatus occurred in the basket flow. After an interval, a few more came back into the shop, then no more. It seemed as though Alf's not being able to stop was turning into his not being able to continue. His wife told me that he had always used the traditional basket-weaver's posture, of sitting on or very near the floor, but that was getting impossible for him to do.

After shutting the baskets away I went for a damp, drizzly wander, getting so wet it might just as well have been raining properly. Over the wide view, the stormy sky was filled with a great twisting flourish of grey cloud, such as Hokusai might have loved. A slow rabbit was at the top of the track. It scarcely moved to get away. I think it may have been the last rabbit I have seen there.

❧

When the damson trees had started producing more fruit than we could eat, I had set forth in hope, thinking organic damsons would be snapped up in North London. The friendly fruiterer in Belsize Park shattered this illusion by saying, 'People don't know what damsons are, if you'd brought me Victorias that'd be different'.

Although Victoria plums are indeed delicious, they do deserve to be called Common. Damsons are even more delicious, but with them the story is of a long, post-war descent in obscurity. Blue-black, with a slight bloom, they are strong, astringent, and somehow dark-tasting. In her book, *Damsons*, Sarah Conrad Gothie quotes a recent, apt description by Kevin West of damsons as 'everything twenty-first century fruit is not: small, sour and demanding'.

There we have it, sweetness conquers all. The damson, an ancient, tart fruit, is becoming a taste of the past. In the approximate world of describing tastes, wines made with old Bordeaux grapes such as Malbec and Carménère are likened to damsons: deep, rich, acidic, while the more popular Merlot is called plummy. These old vines (Carménère is among the most ancient of European varieties) were taken from France, notably to Chile and Argentina, before the mid-nineteenth-century disaster of phylloxera. So they, and their 'damson notes', survive.

Prunus insititia is the damson's Latin name, which refers to its use as a rootstock for grafting. Botanists have disagreed about whether it is a species in its own right, or a subspecies. Where damsons come from is also debatable. Their name suggests Damascus and there is a romance that thirteenth-century crusaders brought them back, but damson stones have been found in Roman and pre-Roman rubbish pits in various European countries, including Britain.

As in the westward journey of the apple, Alexander the Great probably helped move the damson, by taking his armies into Persia, famed for its orchards. Which does not mean we have to imagine soldiers carefully carrying plants home (as they did with snowdrops, during the Crimean War). Because, says Barrie Juniper, in a wonderful book, *The Story of the Apple*, 'the movement of men and horses could not have failed to move fruit seeds of all kinds'.

After the difficulty with selling fresh damsons, I found another way to use them. Every autumn I go in for a lot of weighing, boiling, sieving, sterilizing and labelling to make pickle for a shop in Kentish Town. The shop owner said he could not sell the fresh fruit but then spoke wistfully of his grandmother's damson pickle. That he could sell, he thought. Over time, for the love of variety, I had added damson jam, jelly and cheese. Making them takes far too long to be economically viable, but it is fun, and may help a forgotten fruit find new admirers.

❧

The weather was better, and there was plenty of time to strim under the damson trees before the picking team arrived from Bath. Earlier in the year I had doubted there would be much fruit, but there was, even though some of it was split. Apparently, erratic bouts of hot, then rainy weather cause splitting. There is not much to be done about that. Also, there is the heavy clay. The places famous for growing damsons, Cumbria and Shropshire, may have better drainage.

We picked until lunchtime, filling boxes as well as the baskets. The idea had been to return later to do some more. After a good lunch beside the river this no longer seemed so pressing. Instead, I could dangle the prospect of an outing.

Low Ham, a tiny nearby settlement, has a more intriguing past than meets the eye. Although I cannot put my finger on why I should feel this, the escarpment of which the wood is part also gives me the sense of a hidden, possibly linked, past. To my pleasure, a local historian expressed a similar idea. The fact that the Somerset Archaeological and Natural History Society was putting on a day of lectures about Low Ham was therefore an exciting prospect.

I had already invited Martin and Louise to join me for the 'History Day' but the programme did not include a site visit. So it was easy to forsake damsons and set off in search of the ghosts of a Roman villa and two seventeenth-century mansions.

In 1998, when I was looking for land in the vicinity, my first chosen fields lay beyond Low Ham. I had quite often passed one part of it, a few farms and houses along a quiet road. There is another separate part I rarely saw, with a small surprising church. Next to a farmyard but otherwise isolated, it stands below rising, terraced pastureland. No graveyard, no yew trees, no saintly dedication, just a church, left out like a forgotten toy. As with the rose garden along the woody lane, this church took on an elusive quality, in that I could only find it sometimes. It was coming across its endearing name, 'The Church in the Field' that confirmed that it really did exist.

The parish magazine listed occasional services there, so the next time I could go, I checked the map and went. It was Easter, wild and wet. It looked as though parking in the farmyard was all right, then came some hopping through mud and puddles to reach a path leading to an old, seemingly locked door. As far as electric fences would allow, I looked for other doors, then came back and knocked on the original one. Leaning an ear to the lock, nothing was to be heard from inside.

A moment of waiting . . . then came a rasping sound. As if the door had been closed for centuries, it juddered open. I was welcomed in by a woman, exclaiming, 'I thought there was someone there, not just the wind!' We tiptoed further in, she gave me a hymn book and then I joined a congregation of, perhaps, five.

My first impression was of somewhere austere, with a kind of grandeur even though it was small. White stone effigies of a couple lying on their backs on top of their tomb took up a fair chunk of the space. The air felt damp, with the sound of rain falling on corrugated iron in some intermediate part of the roof. No rain fell on us, but neither did it sound to be very far away.

An old lady sat at the harmonium looking cold, a drip on the end of her nose. But the positive warmth and energy of the rector swept all chill aside as she related how she had been up for the pre-dawn vigil, then hither and yon among the many parishes she serves. Now this was the last Easter service of the day and everything was joy and hope. Of course we would sing, all six of us. And we did, with, or maybe against, the voice of the harmonium.

In the face of this buoyant spirit even the rain had stopped by the time the rector was waiting for us outside the door. One moment she was standing, robes billowing, the next a big dog came bounding up with an enthusiastic muddy-pawed greeting, smack on the front of her white surplice. I got the impression that it was her dog, and husband, there to accompany her back to Langport.

The Church in the Field, with its eccentricity, its air of hanging on by a thread, its commendably short services, suited me well, being only a residual sort of churchgoer. I managed to attend a couple of services there, but then its elusive quality set in again. This time it was no longer that it seemed to move about, but that no more services were listed. The windswept notice by the farm gate was vague about what was happening. Then some scaffolding appeared at one end of the church.

I feared the worst. Because, however unreasonable it is, I want churches to stay open, even while not wanting to be a good, loyal parishioner. In the same vein, it is a comfort to read that the Ladies' Sewing Circle or the Scrabble Club are still there, just in case. The thought of a heritage makeover was less appealing, to me, than the sound of rain on corrugated iron.

When Martin and Louise and I arrived on that September afternoon and read a more recent notice on the farm gatepost, it was clear things had moved on. We were welcome, we were to look for the church key on another gatepost, and lock up after our visit . . . so far, so good. Handsome cattle, dark brown, grey and white, buff and white, some with long curly horns, were sitting next to the path to the church door. They made no difficulty in letting us pass.

The church is now in the care of The Churches Conservation Trust, and has been lovingly restored. There is information about its past, as a quasi-private chapel, and four cut-out Perspex shapes propped up on pews, representing Sir Edward Hext and his wife, the ones lying on their tomb, and Lord Stawell and his wife, who were of the same family, two generations on. These Royalist gentry are central to the chapel's story, and that of its vanished mansions.

Any faint draught from their ghosts that might still have been there in the time of the chapel's dilapidation is now gone. Sound stonework, a watertight roof and laminated questions aimed at primary school visitors seem to have driven them away.

However, their chapel is still consecrated and they, given the short lifespan of their houses, might be amazed and pleased that it has not been allowed to fall down. Another thing that might comfort them is the fact that we still have a monarch. Even I, though more attuned to the soft and crumbling than to the spick and span, am glad their chapel has not been allowed to fall down.

We locked up but were not finished, because there were the remains of a grand garden, possibly two grand gardens, to try to trace in the grassy terracing, and speculation to be enjoyed about where the houses had stood. I had not been on to this land before because there seemed no access, but now we were invited to pick our way over a stile and walk up towards the one built feature that is still visible, a high stone wall. It runs up from the farm buildings to the brow of the hill, then turns right to reach the lane, enclosing the pasture on two sides. Tumbledown in places, but still very much a wall, the wonder is that so much potential building stone was not 'liberated' long ago. Most of the fabric of the houses, by contrast, went untraceably away.

It was a surprise, on scrambling over loose masonry in a low point of the wall, to see not only many more of the handsome cattle, but also good views of the countryside. The climb up from the church had been gradual, not enough to give a sense of gaining height. Assuming this to be the garden wall, it was intriguing to think of those seventeenth-century garden-makers firmly shutting out the sort of view that their successors would soon be keen to throw open.

However, the times you live in make all the difference to the way you look at things. People only a generation or so older than William Kent, who famously 'saw that all nature was a garden', had experienced scarcely imaginable disruption, before, during and after the Civil War. It probably made them appreciate a high wall better than an open view.

The ground of the pasture is full of bumps with a few scrubby bushes, some trees and a smoother way up the middle. The grass terraces are towards the lane, and on the other side of the smoother central way. The chapel lies lower down, with the farm. Of the three of us, Louise was alone in suggesting a plan of how things might have been laid out, but I was not sure I could follow it properly.

All that the grass terraces murmured to me was that it is hard to move earth, so once they were there, they had stayed put, but no images came floating up of what might have grown on them, or why it had been worth the initial effort to make them. Martin stood looking out over the landscape at a distant church, which he supposed to be in quite a different place from where I supposed it to be.

This all added up to a very cheerful expedition. We enjoyed it, and looked forward to hearing more. I got some inkling of what might have been passing in my brother's mind as he was taking in the view, when he announced that they would set off from there without consulting the map, and just wander.

Before saying goodbye we stood by some railings with a notice about the site of the Roman villa. (A notice of which, subsequently, it appears I may have dreamt.) It struck me that this part of Low Ham, so modest, so unremarkable, just a farm and a few houses, was very good at playing down its secrets.

∾

Once the damsons were picked it was the turn of the apples and pears. Even in a bad year, as this one partly was because of a late frost in the first orchard, there are still a lot. I ask Hecks Cider Farm of Street to press them into juice. Somerset villages, despite all the Orchard Closes and Apple Tree Ways around their outskirts, are still awash with apples. Hecks are so busy with pressing thousands of them that each customer only gets one go.

This means I have to find somewhere to store the early ripeners, while the later ones catch up. The only place where the rats do not eat them is the cottage, so that becomes more and more fragrant as the season progresses. All this, being done in fits and starts, lasts into October. But it was still only mid-September when I was sweeping the Rollalong, prior to leaving for London.

Much to my surprise, two young policemen appeared. It is very rare for any unexpected visitor to turn up at the Rollalong, let alone the police. Perhaps it was the dustpan and brush in my hands that made one of them ask if I lived there. Soon they explained their business, which was to do with sheep. They were trying to trace the owner of about thirty of them, found on the loose up the hill. Immediately I thought of the wool on the barbed wire, and how, being sure she would not worry about it, I had not warned Laura that a few of hers knew how to get out. The policemen talked of thefts of stock in the neighbourhood. I gave them her phone number and off they went.

On the journey back to London I was trying to imagine Laura's sheep (if the ones on the loose were Laura's) struggling up the thicketed slope. As domesticated animals, it seemed strange that they would bother, unless for the love of freedom. The way animals do manage to escape the gates, fences, pens, doors we use to confine them, makes me think that they do love freedom. Before humankind became so dominant, the forebears of domestic animals had whole continents to cross. We are told that they move on in search of water and food and to escape predators, but I suspect there is more to it than that.

This led me on to thinking, in relation to Aller Hill, of 'green corridors'. Green corridors are what wildlife need, in our over-concreted world, to get from one patch of land where they can still live, to another. I wondered how easy it is for the wild creatures, from rodents to deer and badgers, to travel along the whole, often overgrown escarpment of Aller Hill, whether its few miles count as a green corridor, and if those that can fly need a corridor at all. A brief thought of trying it in an earthbound way myself, battling through the undergrowth in the name of research, was easy to lay aside. There is a public footpath most of the way, which the animals could presumably use just as easily as we can.

The paths the deer make, of which there are several through the wood and across the nearby fields and ditches, make it seem as though they are not much troubled by obstacles. There are at least two places where their paths lead to greenery so thick it looks impenetrable, and yet the paths do not deviate. When I got home there was a text from Laura saying that the lost sheep were not hers. I went to bed with a lighter heart.

medlars on a tea towel

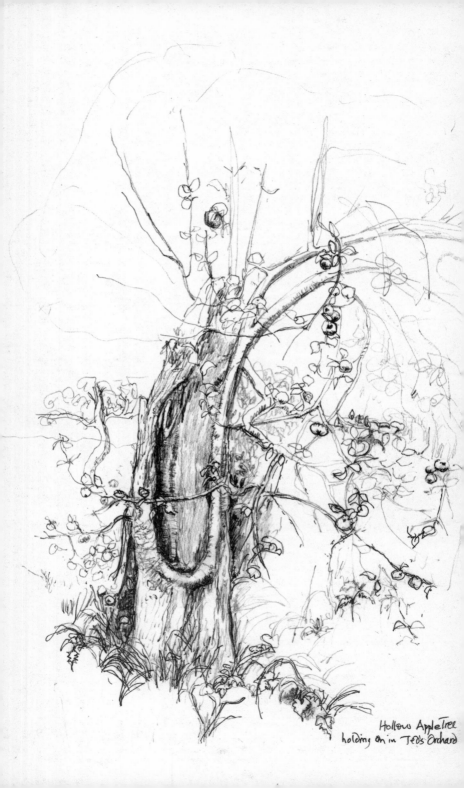

Hollow Apple Tree
holding on in Ted's Orchard

*From the Autumnal Equinox,
past the Winter Solstice
(almost to New Year)*

The men of the forest
they askit of me
How many strawberries
grow in the salt sea?
I askit them back with
a tear in my e'e,
How many ships sail
through the forest?

From The Unfaithful Bride, *a folksong sung by*
Emma Overd of Langport to Cecil Sharp in 1904

I N LATE SEPTEMBER, AS A GUEST of the Langport Over
Sixties Club, I heard Emma Overd's great-great-grand-
daughter, Linda Elphick, singing this song to illustrate the
talk that her mother, Shirley Nicholas, was giving.

Shirley has served on the Parish Council of Huish Episcopi for
decades. Despite being well-qualified to do so, it only occurred
to her lately that joining an Over Sixties Club might be fun. She
tried it, reconnected with school friends, and became a member.
Soon she was asked to give a talk about the council, but she
preferred to talk about her great-grandmother.

Striking photographs were up on the screen in the pavilion
where the club meets. They were taken by Cecil Sharp, who
wanted to record the singers as well as the songs. These show
Emma Overd and her neighbours/relations outside their
row of cottages near the river in Westover, Langport. The
women look plainly dressed but pleased to be photographed.
The cottages look as rural cottages used to look, when poor
working people occupied them. This particular row has been

demolished, but had it been still there it would have been prettied up by now.

Mrs Overd stands at her door in the sunshine, her strong, willow-worker's hands clasped over a smooth snowy apron. One sleeve of her patterned dress is rolled up, the other loose, so she has not taken a huge amount of trouble to present herself to Cecil Sharp's camera.

She was no longer young when he took the picture; she could have been a member of the Over Sixties Club for years, had any such thing existed. Instead, there was a pub she liked in Westover. She looks confident. As well she might, the vigorous, accomplished singer that she was. If she had any explanation of that riddle about strawberries and ships in the wrong places, her expression suggests that she might have thought it too obvious to bother with.

Shirley was soon into her story, mentioning in passing that a descendant of another of the singers who sang to Cecil Sharp was in the audience. Among the songs that Linda sang was 'Green Bushes', which, like 'The Unfaithful Bride', concerns a fickle young maid and a sorrowing lover. In those I have heard her sing before it is often the other way round, the men heartless and the girls forsaken. Some folk singers are very forceful in their rendering of such tales but Linda sings with a veiled melancholy, which I prefer.

It is hard to date folk songs but some of those in Emma Overd's repertoire would surely have been known in the century before hers, when Anna Maria and Elizabeth Sugg lived their short lives and most of their children died before having the chance to grow up. It is no wonder that folk songs, of love, loss, partings, ships and the salt sea are often so full of lament.

After Shirley had finished, the woman in charge of proceedings (with whom I had had a previous word) announced my interest in memories of Aller. The audience was breaking up when a smiling man approached, making a passage through the rows of wooden chairs, and introduced himself as David Crossman. His mother, he said, had grown up in Aller. She was no longer living there in his time, but had told him how she would walk from Aller to Langport to go to school (a fair way for a child, twice a day). Immediately, with my interest in paths, I asked which way she went, along the road, or perhaps by a shorter route over the fields and along the river, on footpaths now lost?

This degree of detail, unsurprisingly, had not been passed down. David began talking of his great-great-uncle, Frederick Crossman, the singer Shirley had said was another of Cecil Sharp's contributors. Frederick Crossman, market gardener, singer, bell-ringer of Huish Episcopi, was clearly a live wire; he is still remembered for singing and joining in the bell-ringing at his own wedding.

David said that another part of his family goes back to the twelfth century on Exmoor, and that a book has been written about them. At which I could only wish that it was in Aller that they had lived all that time. Exmoor is a fascinating and singular area but not one that I could, by any stretch of imagination or fancied movement of underground water, include here.

After Shirley's talk it was time to pick more apples. Distant owl hoots came sailing down from the higher ash wood as I left. This has now happened often enough for me to hope that the time of not hearing them at all may be over. I thought they might have gone, for lack of rabbits. Perhaps if the owls are back it says something good about numbers of other small creatures, the fate of which it is to be swept up by talons and eaten.

The only owl I have ever actually seen nearby was a barn owl. It gave me a shock, swooping out of what was in Ted's day the ponies' stable, which Philip has now turned into the bungalow. Ted said he had seen the barn owl a few times, then no more. Barn owls are beautiful, it would be thrilling to have resident ones. To me, though, they are like the white admiral butterflies, in that I never expected them to be there. The tawny owls were always there, give or take some quiet times of the year, so to have them back feels like a reprieve. Now, thanks to Roger the ornithologist and his suggested nesting box, I can start dreaming of little owls as well.

Apples and pears took up the rest of that visit. There was one thing I was very pleased to see before leaving for London . . . the autumn crocus, in all its pale mauve glamour and improbability. There are autumn-flowering crocus that really are crocus, but the ones known as Autumn Crocus, or Naked Ladies, are not. They are colchicums instead. As the expert, Christine Skelmersdale, says, 'Colchicums seem to have more than their fair share of names – most of them wrong'. Calling them Naked has sense to it though, in that the leaves and flowers come up at completely different times, leaves in spring, flowers in autumn.

The Naked Lady along the boundary walk is a double one called 'Waterlily'; elegant, sophisticated, and, I admit, an odd choice for its rough surroundings. From Skelmersdale's descriptions, Meadow Saffron would have been better, because it grows wild throughout Europe, including Britain. So that is one to try. Meanwhile, I love my misplaced lady, and am always pleased to see her.

❧

Extinction Rebellion activists were out in London when I next left for Somerset. I tried a more suburban route than usual, only to find a parallel universe; the streets blocked by big 4 x 4 vehicles picking up small children from school. Maybe the activists were in the wrong place . . .

From the Autumnal Equinox, past the Winter Solstice

The slow journey had me pondering who was worse, those school-run mums with cloth ears, or me who could hear the Rebels' message, but still drives. If I had found out two decades ago how tortuous the public transport links are between London and Langport, I might have looked for better-connected land. Now my trees are planted and my heart is in the wood. It is also in London, inconveniently enough.

Laura of the sheep had sent a message to say that she had seen people going in and out of the wood, and that the caravan had been stolen from outside the bungalow. It seemed unlikely that anyone would bother to steal the Rollalong, but it was still good to rediscover it, unmolested, in its green bower. Further up in the Disputed Territories were less encouraging signs; a path roughly cut through land that the Land Registry plan says is mine. I took some pictures, determined to contact my cousin again, and tried to shake off the unease caused by this wordless dispute.

After that it was more of a pleasure than usual to revert to picking hard pears and talking to errant sheep. I sent Laura a picture of two of them in possession of the boundary walk, to which she replied 'Little Monsters . . . they clearly remember your field!' I had been looking out in vain for Wonky in Philip's orchard, so was glad when Laura reported that she was fine, but up at the farm.

There were fairy ring mushrooms popping up in the grass, bracket fungus on the big hazel, various other fungi. One, shiny with rain and surrounded by low nettles, had a great bite out of it as in a cartoon, and a blush-pink one was sprouting from dead elm wood. I paused over a few looking like edible field mushrooms, but was doubtful about the smell of them.

Once the apples and pears were at Hecks for juicing, it was time to transplant some slender apple grafts from their nursery bed in the cottage garden. One is from the Hermit's Apple, two from trees I had only ever named by their position along the boundary walk, 2nd Along, 3rd Along, etc., a system not improved by some of the parent trees falling down. When I dug holes for the trees, up came small, bright white lumps of stone. Following a recent visit to Bowdens Quarry, I inspected them for fossils.

The quarry is a short way along the escarpment, a source of White, Blue and Grey Lias stone. (Why the blue, which is grey, is called blue is no more obvious than why horses called grey are white. There must have been a lot of shifting in the perception of white/grey/blue.) In my time, the quarry has sometimes been in operation, sometimes closed, but the company Lovell Stone has been at work there since 2011. It was then 'just a field', says its website. I went in to ask if they knew anything about the spring line along the escarpment.

It is odd to see an area of the hill you know as grassy or wooded stripped bare of its green clothing, and doubtless worse than odd to the wildlife that was using it. On either side of the approach road all is stony pale, with a mass of blocks piled down the slope. Everywhere was white dust and glare. The noise of stonecutting came from one end of the building, but I approached its office end. There was no one there, so I nosed into the cutting enclosure. Stopping work, taking off protective headgear and ear defenders, a man politely took me into the office.

He was the quarry foreman. As I had not come to order any stone I felt bad about interrupting him, but ploughed on with my story nonetheless, springs, pond, Mendip and all. The reception room is like a museum, full of samples of stone, not just of Lias but of others from quarries within the company, Purbeck stone, Bath stone, Green Hurdstone. There are photographs of fossils, quarried out of their long repose on Aller Hill.

A couple of local geologists like to call in now and then in case of anything interesting, the foreman said. About water, they had found two Roman wells on the site (aha) and in one place water oozes up from the pile of cut stones. As to an actual spring, he was not sure, adding that the water that comes up from the borehole is very hard.

He showed me photographs of the fossilised dragonfly he found, which is now in Bristol Museum. He was modest about it, but the Lovell Stone website is more enthusiastic, describing it as rare, exceptionally well preserved, perhaps of a previously unrecorded species. I thought of the dragonflies around the pond, hoping to see some likeness. All dragonflies look spindly, but the one turned into stone looked much spindlier, as though it had been made up of only a few threads.

Several late Triassic fossils have been found in the quarry and given to museums, including an ichthyosaur. From the look of ichthyosaurs in pictures, I would not like to find one of them in the pond. How many more fossils have been missed, even by sharp-eyed quarrymen, is anyone's guess.

If this visit to the quarry was among my last pursuits of the water-from-Mendip-idea, and I accept that the water in the pond has not come far, I would still like to understand more about the spring. There is a spring marked on the Ordnance Survey map of 1901, above the old chapel in Aller . . . But this will o' the wisp, and others in the form of the Roman wells and a nearby Saxon burial site, are for another time.

Meanwhile, as I looked at the fragments of white lias from the apple-planting holes and paused over some faintly raised lines, the possibility of their representing anything fossilised or rare seemed remote. They are still handsome, so I placed them as markers for the daffodils from Ron Scamp around the grafted trees, all unawares that the subject of White Lias would soon come up again, in a different context.

∾

The day arrived for the talks about Low Ham, organised by the Somerset Archaeological and Natural History Society. We were to hear about the two lost mansions and their people, some local nature reserves, the Church in the Field, the gardens of the mansions, the original excavation of the Roman villa, and then more recent excavations of the site.

It was a good programme and well-attended. As the day progressed, however, I did begin to wonder if some of the speakers might share my own, late-in-the-year feeling, that their buried, conjectural subjects had not yet fully revealed themselves.

The nature reserves had the advantage of not being conjectural. Their immediate former lives, often as peat diggings, are within living memory and their current purposes are clear; to provide habitat for wetland species, in a landscape that has lost much of its marshes, bogs and ponds. As an example of how providing the right conditions works, we were shown a picture of the rare Large Marsh Grasshopper. Standing on green pond leaves, it looks sporty in its clear colours; green/black body, yellow/black legs with red flash, fawn wings with a netting-like pattern. Listed as our biggest grasshopper, it survives mainly around the bogs of the New Forest, so its presence on the Somerset Levels is a thing to celebrate.

The Church in the Field is not lost either, but we soon heard how conjectural its past is, starting with the time of its building. Our speaker thinks that it may have been meant, nostalgically, to look as though it belonged to a previous age, making it hard to date what is actually there. Whoever ordered its construction would be among those included in the next talk, *A Fool and his Money* . . .

This was about the successive generations of Sir Edward Hext's family, whose surname soon changed to Stawell through his daughter's marriage. They caused one mansion, and then another, and at some point the chapel, to be built. The first house was pulled down, the second fell down, which makes the survival of their isolated chapel, the Church in the Field, the more remarkable.

The Stawell title had been upgraded when the moment came to reward royalist loyalty, so Sir John Stawell's son became Ralph, Lord Stawell. By the time he died in 1689, the second mansion was taking shape. It was built to the north of the church, we heard, where the farm buildings are. Not the most alluring site, as it seems to me, but in accord with Louise's earlier thoughts.

To be fair, the 'fool and money' title may mainly refer to John Stawell (the 'profligate baron') who died, aged twenty-three, in 1692, leaving large debts and the second mansion unfinished. With estates all over the south-west and remarriages, it is unclear if any subsequent members of the Stawell family really lived in the still unfinished house, or enjoyed the fruits of the work of so many labourers, craftsmen, gardeners. It was very grand, supposedly the grandest house in Somerset. The widow of the Lord John Stawell who died so young went in for energetic asset-stripping.

Perhaps after that the house became a white elephant, best forgotten, although local court sessions were held on the ground floor later on . . . it takes time, after all, for the rain to penetrate everywhere, for elaborate plaster or painted ceilings to collapse, for ash saplings to sprout indoors. There seem to be no drawings to show what the house looked like. A known surviving feature, a gateway arch, was removed to Sparkford where, much more recently, it suffered the new indignity of being cut off from the house it was meant to enhance by the building of the A303. It gives little away about what was lost 'in a vast pile of a stately ruin'.

Deeper Into the Wood

Of the several topics connected with seventeenth-century Low
Ham, I particularly wanted to understand more of the gardens.
We were shown aerial photographs, which made the lumps and
bumps on the ground look more organised than when we had
walked over them a few weeks before. Not organised enough,
however, to make gardens spring up in the imagination. The
speaker invited us to picture the smoother, track-like sweep in
the middle as perhaps having led from a house up at the highest
point of the land. Although this idea is unpopular with other
commentators, I liked that picture; it looks a more exciting place
to have a house than tucked below the church. He also mentioned
the planting of avenues of trees. Only think of the effort of it,
the earthworks, the planting, the watering, and all for nothing.

If some of the labourers were local, they might have been able
to observe the abandoned gardens maturing into a wilderness
with, let us guess, fancy foreign trees newish to the countryside.
Or, in a preferable fantasy, have helped themselves to saplings
early on. They might then have been able to sit out their old
age under a Spanish chestnut, a cedar of Lebanon, a Turkish
sycamore. Never mind that those labourers would not have had
planting land, or have been likely to reach old age. The unlikely
does, after all, sometimes come about . . .

At stages of the day, I found myself thinking, why not just
dig down and look? To which the response must be, it costs too
much. The last speakers were archaeologists, one relating the
original discovery of the remains of the Roman villa, the second
two speaking of their recent muddy weeks in search of more
information about it. Badgers have been making free with the
former facilities of the villa, we heard, specifically, those to do
with underfloor heating.

The most spectacular find from the villa was the first to come
to light, soon after the Second World War; a mosaic pavement

linked to the bath house. Depicting the story of Dido and Aeneas, its discovery caused a sensation. Later, it was moved to Taunton Museum.

No such sensation rewarded our speakers' efforts, but they did find traces of three prehistoric roundhouses. So Low Ham has been chosen as a place to live for a very long time. A sheltered position and the near presence of spring water could account for that, the archaeologists said. The most interesting thing, to my ears, was that Lionel Walrond, of Pitney, had played a part in discovering the mosaic. Walrond is the surname of Rob the organic farmer and his wife, Lizzie, of Pitney Farm Shop.

When I was next there I reported the mention of Lionel Walrond . . . 'that's Uncle Lionel!' was Lizzie's delighted response, adding that he was over ninety, still going strong, and to ask Rob about him. I soon heard from Rob that his uncle, while still only seventeen, had not just been part of the story of finding the mosaic, he had been essential to it, even if that fact had been overlooked by the more senior archaeologists who subsequently took over.

It was, however, Herbert Cook, of the farm, who had made the first discovery. In 1938, when digging a grave for a sheep, he turned up a small tile with unusual combed markings. Somerset Museum staff thought it interesting, but the enquiry was stalled until 1945. Lionel Walrond read about it, and wanted to seek what else might lie below the ground.

Although seven years is a long interval, especially when it includes a major war, Herbert Cook had evidently not forgotten where he buried his sheep. It was the young Lionel, said Rob, who had been able to work out how best to approach what might be underneath. How could he know? I asked. Rob was not sure, other than that Lionel was thoughtful and clever . . .

And alive, and living in Stroud . . . I could feel my allegiance to seventeenth-century Low Ham pivoting towards

The Bracket Fungus on the old Hazel

The Old Hazel with
Bracket Fungus beginning to grow

Romano-British/1945 Low Ham as I asked Rob if he thought I could meet Lionel. Rob was himself meaning to go over to Stroud before Christmas, and said I could go too.

Rob is always busy, so I knew that this date might be hard for him to arrange. In the event, it was not Rob's schedule that prevented me from meeting Lionel Walrond. It was that, as with Alf Brewer the willow-basket weaver, a ninety-year-old can be going strong one moment . . . in hospital the next. Then there was time needed to recover, then Christmas, then things were not looking good . . .

⁂

Rain, rain, go away, Come again another day

⁂

Wet, windy weather was blustering its way through much of autumn, but when I first entered the wood in November all was calm, clear and sunny. A robin was singing, long-tailed tits flitted after each other through plum trees, the leaves were turning colour. Lapped in this midday tranquillity, I was not expecting the sight that was waiting just the other side of the wooden gate into the hazel wood.

Normally on a bright November day, if you stand and look up into the hazel branches, the yellowing leaves of this year and the pale green tightly bunched catkins of next show up together against fragments of blue sky. This time there was a birds-eye view of the treetop bursting straight into my face from ground level, a frothing tangle of leaves, catkins, twigs

181

and lichen blocking the way up to the clearing. One of the old multi-trunked hazels was down.

I skirted the edge of the leafy heap and came to the trunks. Three-quarters of them lay splayed outwards from the rotten base, the rest were still standing in a leggy clump. A couple of young shoots stood upright, as though nothing had happened, but inside the dark browns and blacks of the torn bark was a cauldron of softish, flaky, yellow mush. It looked as though a recipe for something delicious and fluffy had gone irretrievably wrong.

Bracket fungus attached to the outside had been hinting at this inner state of affairs, but had disappeared from view under the ruin of which it was part. Or semi-ruin, as the whole tree still appeared to be alive. Not knowing how long ago it had fallen, I was unsure how to interpret the fact that it was looking sprightly, if horizontal. Among what had been the high branches, the grey-green lichen was looking wonderful. The sight of it had previously been reserved for the squirrels, birds and any other creature that could get up there, but now its fantasy of grey-green lace had descended to my level.

Ever since the energetic amount of clearing up done after the Great Storm, there has been much said about how that effort was misdirected, how it would have been better if more trees had been left where they fell, to allow benign natural processes to lead to regeneration. My understanding of what these benign processes might be is sketchy, but any talk of doing good by doing nothing suits me.

Some of the branches of the hazel had fallen close to the old apple, Arthur Rackham 1, but not reached it. Apart from littering the open space, the hazel would only need trimming on one side to allow a passageway. It could then, so I hoped, be left to itself to go on living, or not.

It did not then seem inevitable that the remaining upright quarter of the tree would fall, but sometime between that visit

Young Cedar dancing
with (much older) Field Maple

and the next, down came the last trunks. Lying up the slope this time, they occupied a fair bit more ground and altered the route for the passageway. No one would say that the view into the hazel wood is as alluring as it was before.

Nevertheless, I was hoping that some of the benign processes of rot and regeneration might be at work and, preferably, visible. For instance, that interesting beetles might move in. So far, on visits to look inside the fallen trunks, a dramatic and compelling sight, I have not seen anything move. Maybe the processes are too small to see. As time has gone by, however, the tree has clearly been active, turning its shoots from horizontal to something approaching vertical, sending up straight new ones. Bracket fungus has reappeared too.

The Rollalong door was propped open on that November day, as I went for my customary wander around . . . loving the place, hearing the occasional bird, noting far more things to do than would ever get done. On my return a robin was flying about inside the Rollalong, blundering against the window. As soon as I entered it dropped down into the inaccessible gloom under the table. The only thing I could think to do was to put up the blind, untouched since the days of sleeping there, and leave the door open. It worked, there was no robin later on. Over the years there has been a greater range of wildlife making use of the Rollalong than I might have wished, but that is the first bird I have ever seen in there.

Up in the higher orchard I planted more bulbs and cleared a tithe of the weeds that grow inside the wire tree guards. Although undoing those guards properly, only to have to fasten and peg them down all over again is so tedious I hardly ever do it, on this occasion there was one grafted tree I was suspicious about. The flourishing growth above the inner, spiral guard looked as if it might be from the rootstock rather than the desired scion of 'Cottage Best'.

So, untwiddled and off and up came the wire guard. The relationship between stock and scion looked all right, but something else unorthodox was going on. In place for too long, the dark dampness of the plastic spiral was encouraging hopeful white rootlets to sprout all the way up. I felt bad about the young tree putting so much energy into roots it did not need.

Rooks were coming home, filling up the former quiet with their conversations. In the slanting sun the cedars, still taller than they are wide, looked like military dancing partners for the more curvaceous field maples, with their butterscotch and golden leaves. The sky remained cloudless and the night brought frost (in retrospect, a rarity). But it was in Yorkshire that the weather took over, bringing not frost but rain, flood and destruction.

It was a new chapter of a story already unfolding, of a wet, wet warm winter, when houses were flooded and growers could not get on to the land. Meanwhile in Australia, a dry, dry summer was leading to fire and catastrophe. Neither of these is surprising. Professor Gabi Hegerl, quoted by the BBC, spells it out, 'The overall climate signal is that if you have it warmer it is easier to burn . . . if you have more moisture in the atmosphere, caused by higher temperatures, the same rainfall systems rain harder . . . in extreme events, that's where climate change bites us.'

∾

The night was frosty but proper stay-indoors rain had set in by the morning, so I went into Taunton Museum to see the Low Ham mosaic. At the entrance we were given plastic bags for dripping umbrellas. I was leaning over to look at the mosaic when a polite attendant pointed out that my bagged umbrella was projecting over it. After all those centuries of lying safe under damp pastureland the risks of being under a bagged umbrella did seem comical . . .

The mosaic, made in about 350 CE, shows five scenes from Virgil's story of Dido and Aeneas. The first image to be scraped back into the light in 1945 shows a rider, identified as Aeneas. He is out hunting, his cloak flying behind him. Apart from the cloak, headgear and boots, he looks underdressed for a horseman, as does the rider behind him, Dido, Queen of Carthage.

Dido, who appears in four of the panels, never wears much. Venus, in her two appearances, wears only a sprinkling of jewellery. The presence of Venus is explained by her being Aeneas's mother. In forwarding her son's interests, she has much to answer for in Dido's tragedy. The other men, blown off course with Aeneas on their way home from Troy, are sitting low in the boats so we only see their faces and Phrygian hats.

In Virgil's tale, one thing leads to another. Venus sees to it that Dido and Aeneas fall for each other, a storm interrupts the hunt, they shelter alone in a cave (or in the mosaic version, between trees). Even there, the allocation of clothing and nakedness is unequal. Aeneas, as though already prepared to desert Dido as his fate demands, presses her bare flesh up against uncomfortable-for-her-looking military attire.

Unless Venus arranged the aftermath too, the only choice Dido seems to have had in the whole matter was how to behave when Aeneas left her. In the cold light of the twenty-first century, sacrificing herself for the sake of a faithless lover does seem more like the act of a silly goose than that of a powerful queen.

In 2013, Lionel Walrond was interviewed by the *Western Daily Press*, about his part, nearly seventy years earlier, in discovering the mosaic. He recalled that, before anything very exciting had been unearthed, it looked as though it was flagstones they were getting to, until he saw a series of lighter flecks against the dark surface. 'I got a scraper, an ancient spoon, and removed nearly a tenth of an inch of limescale . . . I can remember saying . . . it's tesserae, and immediately everyone came down . . . and uncovered part of the second rider. Everyone was excited . . .'

The tesserae used in the mosaic to represent the characters' skin are of White Lias, the same stone as the uncut fragments I had recently dug up while planting apple trees. White Lias also provides a lot of the background, the other colours being terracotta and brownish black. The impression the mosaic makes is of elegant worldliness, created from homely materials.

The white skin tones of the Low Ham pavement look shiveringly northern, but maybe the underfloor heating system of the villa, where the badgers now live, worked well. These villas were built for 'Romano-Britons' rather than Romans. As is usual among empire builders, the Romans subdued the local people, then appointed the leaders of those people to run things for them.

In this case, the locals were of the Durotriges tribe. At first fierce in their opposition to the invaders, with the passage of time their leaders must have come round to the superior comforts of Roman life. They did, clearly, love a villa. As well as at Low Ham, the sites of local villas include High Ham, Pitney, Catsgore, Ilchester, Ham Hill, Westland and Lufton, where Lionel Walrond brought another mosaic to light.

It is thought that the mosaics were made by travelling craftsmen, who took their designs from pattern books. In terms of those mosaics that have survived, have not been damaged or destroyed by ploughing, railway engineering, road-building, Dido and Aeneas at Low Ham is the prize.

With an estimated date of less than a century before the Romans withdrew from Britain, the Low Ham villa was probably short-lived, like the seventeenth-century mansions that came after it. The villa dwellers may have held out for a while as the orderly life around them began to disintegrate, but the level of sophistication that had brought underfloor heating to Somerset could not endure.

A small plate attached to one corner of the Dido and Aeneas mosaic in Taunton says, 'Removal and Restoration by the Marble Mosaic Co. Ltd, Wade Street, Bristol, 1953–54'. This company was started by Romano Maddalena in 1905, so the skilled craftsmen of 350 CE have had their successors. The company continues still, in Weston-super-Mare, but working on a different scale. No more tesserae, instead, it makes architectural precast concrete panels for prestigious building projects.

I contacted the Mosaic Marble Co. Ltd. (MMC) to ask if there was anything in the archive about moving the Low Ham mosaic (which must have been a feat). Stephen Maddalena, grandson of Romano the founder, replied to say that the archives had not survived two moves, but that he knew that MMC had carried out occasional refurbishment work on Roman mosaics in the 1950s and 60s, probably employing the skills of craftsmen from Friuli, who had followed his grandfather to Bristol.

Then his mother reminded him that he was 'an eye-witness to the removal of the Low Ham mosaic. She recalls a family outing to the site and seeing some excavation works in the middle of a field (in early 1953?).' Stephen excuses his failure to recall this by pointing out that he was only a few months old at the time, before adding, 'MMC's involvement in the mosaic must have been special as she didn't usually accompany my father on his site visits'.

Before leaving Somerset I made a final trip to the wood. There were still unpicked apples out of reach on the Reinette d'Ananas but they refused to be shaken off. By contrast, with only a gentle push the pears on Nouveau Poitou came pelting down. Eight days later not a single fruit remained, on the trees or the ground, so it was not just me who had been keeping an eye on them.

❧

You'll forget the little ploughboy,
who whistled o'er the lea . . .

From William Shield's hit number
in the comic opera, The Farmer, 1787

❧

As mentioned before, we are told to forget that particular ploughboy because he is off to London to make his fortune, but by now we have forgotten all the whistling ploughboys. Their few successors are high up in the closed cabs of huge tractors, wearing headphones to enliven the isolation of their long working days.

Farming comes so high up the list of reasons for the decline of Britain's wildlife that I wanted to hear a local opinion on those intertwined matters. Rob Walrond has a finger on this pulse, not only as a farmer himself but through his voluntary activities.

Rob's immediate connection with his family farm in Pitney began when his father took it on in the 1980s. There are photographs displayed in the farm shop of an earlier generation (including a young Lionel Walrond) showing the sort of small farm of which children's books are made. Rob's father had electricity installed in 1983.

Intensive methods, requiring more chemicals and larger machinery, were well on the march during his father's time, but they were not to the advantage of small farms. Intensification 'wasn't adding up', is how Rob put it, of the decision to change to organic methods in the late 1990s. This failure to add up was not just to do with money. There was, Rob said, the question of stewardship of the land, of 'looking after creation'.

He could think of numerous creatures in decline in the immediate countryside. There were, for instance, definitely more hares thirty years ago, the numbers falling off in the last fifteen, and the rabbits have 'crashed'. Local enthusiasm for shooting might have something to do with it, but then there is the dwindling of hedgehogs, starlings, glow-worms, sparrows and thrushes to account for as well. The local shoot can hardly be held responsible for all of those. Badgers might be implicated in the loss of the hedgehogs, Rob said, and there are more flying predators, rooks, ravens and buzzards around.

When they changed to organic methods Rob sowed clover in with the grass and started stocking with native breeds, Aberdeen Angus and Devon cattle, Lleyn sheep, Saddleback pigs, because the animals are more self-sufficient and hardy. But, while organic farming is better for insects, soil life, birds and so on, Rob's land is not continuous . . . with chemical spraying going on in between, some of the benefit is compromised. One local farmer is moving towards using fewer insecticides. But another, well . . . Rob's shrug suggested that although there was more to be said on that subject, he was not going to say it.

Instead he went on, '. . . farming has not had a good press over the years, but if you want food to be cheap, someone has to lose. Most farmers are defensive, feel they're being blamed.'

About which they are not wrong. Here, for instance, is Michael McCarthy, author of *The Moth Snowstorm*, on his generalised figure, Farmer Giles, and the post-war adoption of the wonder chemicals '. . . herbicides, pesticides, fungicides, molluscicides . . . Farmer Giles loved them all, he turned on the tap and let a great flood of poison wash over the land, which, God help us, floods over it to this day.'

Or Mark Cocker, author of *Our Place*. On the same topic of farmers taking up the modern agricultural products, he writes of the 'psychological journey' they made 'from viewing an entire chemical arsenal – herbicides, fungicides and pesticides – as an expensive and technical line of last resort, to a prophylactic standby. Chemical sprays are often deployed regardless of need . . .'

These chemicals that end in '. . . cide' are only part of the story. Of artificial nitrate fertilisers, which increase crop yields but deplete the soil and wash off to pollute the waterways, he writes, '. . . Eventually British farmers could not get enough of them . . .'

In his foreword to *Farming and Birds*, a thorough and devastating study, Ian Newton is judicious towards the farmers. Though he knows all too well the harm to wild plants and animals that agricultural changes have brought, he writes, '. . . it is easy to give the impression of criticising farmers. But this is not my intent. The nation's farmers did an excellent job of what was asked of them . . . and were in no better position than anyone else to foresee the severe environmental consequences'.

Except, one cannot help interjecting, the farmers were *there*, literally on the ground. If they could not have been expected to foresee, they might have noticed and questioned more over the years, as these severe consequences were becoming clearer.

The cynical response would be that farmers were making money, so of course they went for intensification. But the thought that all those people, who have been getting up early every morning of the week over the past six or seven decades to tend livestock and crops, were motivated only by greed is unbelievable. Quite apart from the fact that many of them were getting more into debt than wealth.

Far easier to understand is the story of gradual disillusionment with intensive farming methods, as recorded by James Rebanks. In *English Pastoral*, he describes his family's slow shift from the old ways of farming, through modernization and on to the recognition that the newer methods were leading to ecological mayhem. Of 'good' and 'bad' methods he says, 'We didn't really know when we had crossed the invisible threshold from one to the other'. That sounds all too believable, and could be echoed up and down the country. As could Rebanks's references to the historical distrust between farmers and environmentalists. The latter, as I can recall from occasional remarks made in my cousins' farm kitchen, were as likely to be seen as pestilential do-gooders as helpful advisors.

Among Rob Walrond's voluntary activities is listening to farmers who are, to put it mildly, downhearted. It is well known that they are at particular risk from suicidal depression, and often have the means and solitude to act upon it. Here is Rob's off-the-cuff list of worries he hears about from farmers:

- More extreme weather intervals caused by climate change
- Increased wind blowing in more diseases, e.g. Blue Tongue
- Global capitalism and trade bringing in more diseases
- Pressure from supermarkets
- Pressure from suppliers of chemicals
- Pressure from public opinion
- Uncertainties related to Brexit

I asked Rob if he could think of any encouraging developments. Yes, he could, from a sector of the industry I would not have expected. In most writing about nature conservation, farm machinery is a villain. As it has got bigger and heavier it has been wrecking the soil, squashing it, killing its life forms, leaving no grubs for the birds, etc. But modern tillage and drilling (i.e. ploughing and sowing) methods, said Rob, are being developed to do less damage. He listed 'zero tillage, strip tillage and minimal tillage systems' and was positive about their potential for greater precision of sowing, therefore less disturbance of the 'community of the soil'. In this, they sound somewhat akin to organic gardening's *No Dig* methods.

The last thing I asked Rob was about badgers, Bovine TB and his cattle. 'We've got to get rid of the disease,' he said, then explained some of the intricacies of the regular tests cattle undergo, how the numbers are all important, and sometimes with his herd, worrying. So, in the absence of alternatives he was in support of badger culling. Since our conversation took place the welcome announcement has been made; culling is to be phased out in favour of vaccination.

As far as I can tell, badger culling in Somerset (probably elsewhere too) has had an *Alice in Wonderland* quality to it. Being a protected species, badgers must be left to the free enjoyment of their setts in the breeding season, even if these happen to be where builders want to dig or Network Rail needs to shore up the railway. On the other hand they can, or could, be culled in the hope of limiting the spread of Bovine TB.

If the vaccination programme brings the disease under control, as let us hope it does, it will be intriguing to see if there is a decrease in the number of badger carcasses on roadside verges. They are there, so it is said, because farmers worried about TB shoot badgers (illegally), then place their bodies to make it look as though they have been run over.

I agree with Ian Newton about not intending simply to criticise farmers for the disasters happening to wildlife, particularly those like my cousin's late husband who started work at the beginning of the post-war period of modernization. It was then an exciting era, with the hope that science and technology would at last fix everything, including food production. Food would be made plentiful and cheap. And so it was . . .

Current farmers are in a different, more complicated position. They can hardly help being aware of the bad effects of intensive farming, or of the fact that they are being blamed for damaging the environment. But they are still expected to produce cheap food.

Many species of wildlife may go extinct in Britain unless they are allowed enough continuous, healthy land in which to live. Blaming is easy. But if it makes farmers feel suicidal there surely must be better ways of engaging with them, to try to restore clean water to the fish, enough pollen to the bee, a soil fit for worms to live in . . .

My next visit was to meet James Cross, Head Gardener at the Bishop's Palace at Wells, and therefore guardian of the huge and beautiful American Black Walnut, parent of the sapling now in the wood. Although I know something of the origins of a fair number of my individual trees, no others have sprung from such a grand tree standing in such a grand place, so I wanted to hear more about it, and the garden in general.

Around the Bishop's Palace, where there is no doubt that the water welling up has come from Mendip, there have been gardens since at least the 1200s, with a long succession of bishops taking more or less notice of them. George Henry Law, who left his job as Bishop of Chester to become the Bishop of Bath and Wells in 1824, was one of those who took more notice. He was in his sixties, with a good career and the arrival of a large family of children already accomplished. It would seem that it was time to indulge an interest in the Picturesque.

The garden archives are sporadic, but it is known that by the later 1700s the care of the formal, Dutch-influenced gardens had been falling away. There had been an L-shaped channel fed by the moat. By Bishop Law's time, says James, it had come to nothing much. The Bishop undertook major relandscaping, including the demolition of two walls of the ruined great hall, as it was blocking the view he wished to create. This is the area now called the South Lawn, where he planted a *Ginkgo biloba*, an up-to-the-minute choice. Looking at the remaining walls of the medieval great hall I wondered if the Bishop had been rash. James approves of what he did.

There is no record of the American Black Walnut being planted, or how it came to be chosen, but the approximate date is 1825. It stands in the first part of the garden, into which you enter through the gatehouse over the moat. Its younger companion, added sometime after lightning struck the original tree in the 1950s, is catching up in height, 'planted too close, really,' says James. In the corner is a shop, with café tables and, in autumn, a chalkboard notice saying 'Caution Falling Walnuts!'

Once James had shown me the further areas of the garden and we had parted company, I enjoyed a slow circuit of the tree. Its lightning wound, filled in with something hard, looks as though it might have grown over better if it had been left to itself. I borrowed a café chair and sat down to draw.

It is a magnificent tree. Some of its high, mossy branches meander down in a lolloping way before doing a flick outwards, giving it a playful look. The trunk has divided on its way up, so that it appears thicker at first floor than at ground floor level.

Some of the roots break through the surface of the grass, showing as gnarled, black, mossy rivulets.

November, even on a sunny day, does not encourage sitting still for long, so I went into the shop. There was merchandise featuring a dark tabby cat sitting on one of the outdoor café tables, stately among the cups and teapots. Having seen occasional newspaper photographs of a cat in possession of the nave of the Cathedral, I asked if this was another one. 'Oh no,' came the swift reply, 'she's not a Cathedral Cat, Maisie's the Bishop's Palace Office Cat!' Which goes to show that it is not just in London that cats are good at establishing official positions for themselves.

∾

I went to the wood to make a list of things to ask Steve the gardener to do, one object being to let in more light around the marsh and pond. It was also a moment for noting down possible planting spots for Lombardy poplars. The nursery had said that the bundle of twenty-five saplings they had been unable to supply in the spring was now awaiting me, so a shelved challenge was coming back to life. Although I really only wanted two of them, there were a few more possible poplar places, or would be, with a lot of clearing.

Casting a sour glance over the mass of dead thistles, I thought how much nicer it would look without them. But there were ladybirds to be seen settling in their stalks when I had been up there, bulb planting. Maybe a stand of thistle, dock and fleabane stalks looks just as winter-welcoming, to a ladybird, as a cosy room glimpsed from outside looks to us in late November.

Using long-handled clippers I picked mistletoe for a friend to sell at a Christmas fair. Some of it grows in my old trees but far more in Philip's orchard. Doreen, Philip's mother, tells me to take as much as I can, now that the man who used to harvest it has died.

So I trundled the barrow back and forth, pressed the springy twigs into bundles as I had seen the Mistletoe Man do, then stuffed them into the back of the car. Looking back at the orchard afterwards, you would not know that any mistletoe had been taken.

November was already three-quarters gone, the time of the year when darkness gallops up, so I left quite early for London.

∾

The next time I saw it, Langport was brighter and more sparkly than I have ever seen it before. By chance I had arrived on the afternoon of the Christmas Fair, but there was still enough daylight for a speedy trip to the wood. From the lower gate, the winter red just starting in the willow stems showed like veiled firelight through the gloom. Steve had been in and sawn off some of the branches overhanging the pond, but I put off looking properly till the next day. Owls were hooting, in a tentative sort of way, as I left to enjoy the sparkling town.

One of the orange/red willows overhangs the pond from above and a pussy willow inclines towards it from below. When I was back at the wood the next day I saw that Steve had made piles of the branches he had cut, one red, one silver-grey. Up in the hazel wood was another pile, of yellowish/grey branches he had trimmed from the fallen hazel tree. From these heaps I took some pieces to decorate the cottage, but there was enough left behind to decorate huge halls. The idea of a house with a hall big enough to decorate, as opposed to a passageway cluttered with bicycles, strikes me as the essence of romance.

For that reason, I regret that Bishop Law chose to demolish the south and east walls of the medieval great hall at Wells, 'to make a more picturesque ruin' when he could have projected a new roof. He had, as it happens, already gone through the experience of raising funds to re-roof the monastic church of St Bees, near Whitehaven. On that occasion, a rich mining family needed to redeem its reputation with the Church, so came up with the money. The theological college the Bishop had imagined, the first such beyond Oxbridge, came into being. Maybe he thought that one rescued medieval building is enough for a lifetime.

From the thickness of the two walls the Bishop allowed to remain standing, it looks as though the demolition job in Wells, and the wheeling in of tons of new topsoil, must have had the Palace grounds in uproar in the mid 1820s. Who, I wonder, would have paid for all this work . . .

Bishop Law's landscaping would have taken place a generation before the period in which Anthony Trollope set his novel, *The Warden*. Published in 1855, it is about reformers upsetting the repose of a cathedral city, not least with the then-topical controversy about charitable funding. However, back in the 1820s, maybe nobody would have blinked an eye, whatever the source of the landscaping money.

Not that I wish to insinuate that Bishop Law snatched bread from the poor to favour his garden. All that seems to be known is that he had independent means. Let us assume, then, that his Picturesque project was his gift to himself and the city. And hope that he enjoyed the results, although it is we who come later who benefit most from big landscaping projects, when the dust has settled and the trees have grown. For the American Black Walnut alone, I have much to thank him.

∾

Now that Steve had cut a path past the fallen hazel I could get in to check both Arthur Rackham trees. It was the further one that was the worry. After the companionable July morning that my nephew and I had spent cutting away brambles to let in more air, my last sight of it in the autumn had been discouraging. Then, its recumbent trunk had looked as though it were dying, if not dead. On this December afternoon, it looked simply dead.

I turned to the better, upright trunk. The highest twigs looked sulky, but probably alive. The way to tell is to scratch back the outer skin; green is good, brown is not, but these were out of reach. Months would have to pass before the buds would open, or not.

There was no sign of rabbits anywhere, but plenty of deer tracks, especially down the field edge of the hedgerow, the route I have been wishing to discover had been an old way from the hill to the river. I felt that if the hedgerow could be shown to be ancient, perhaps that made an old track more likely, or vice versa, that an old track implied an ancient hedge. 'Hooper's Rule' is sometimes invoked as a means of telling the age of hedges. On the other hand, it is sometimes dismissed.

Here is Oliver Rackham, after he has credited Max Hooper with reviving the scientific study of hedges in the 1970s . . . 'He is responsible for the famous rule that the number of tree and shrub species in a 30 yard length of hedge is equal to the age of the hedge in centuries . . . this rule works in many areas'.

Well, there are two sorts of elm, plus hazel, field maple, privet, wild rose, elder. Yet I doubt if the raggedy hedgerow is seven hundred years old. It seems to lack the authority such a hedge should have, and is not long enough to apply the test several times, as is recommended. There is, however, certainly the deer track beside it, and deer tend to stick to the same routes, time out of mind.

I must admit to being dissatisfied with my imagined whistling ploughboy coming down the imagined track. It still feels as though there is something historic to be discovered up there, even if it is likely to remain forever lost.

The moon was rising as I left and so was the wind, which turned wild all night.

I went to pick up the twenty-five poplar seedlings, which had very good roots, and placed them in the cottage garden. The nurserywoman repeated her warning about how fast the roots were likely to plunge down, so this heeling in really would have to be temporary. Then I went to see what the wind had been up to in the wood. Nothing much, apparently. Not being there every day I cannot be sure of this, but it seems that when the wind blows and when the trees fall are not necessarily the same time. With more mistletoe, but later than would have been wise, I began the drive back to London.

On that journey, I like to be getting towards the street lights before it gets really dark, but this time night was already falling as I crossed Salisbury Plain. Stonehenge was invisible, the rain was getting heavier, the road was awash but on we all went as fast as ever, lights glaring, windscreen wipers struggling to cope. At least mine were. In Penelope Chetwode's brilliant book about an expedition on horseback, *Two Middle-Aged Ladies in Andalusia*, at least she and the mare were only middle-aged. My car and I might be more accurately described as *Two Rather-More-Than-Middle-Aged Ladies on the A303*.

There is no risk of such a travelogue being written, but I will just say that in both cases, we got home all right. Penelope Chetwode, being a sincere Catholic, may have thanked St Christopher for her safe return. I prefer the idea of guardian angels, particularly as represented in Wim Wenders's film, *Wings of Desire*. Early on in my habit of driving to and from London and Somerset, I picked out the shining gilt angels on top of St Marylebone Parish Church as stand-ins for Wenders's angels. They are always there, to greet on the way out, and on the way back.

∾

As a wintry interlude, I would like to mention something about Samuel Johnson that I came across at this time in Alexandra Harris's *Weatherland*. It feels worth sharing with anyone who, like me, does not achieve a string of things before breakfast in December.

Johnson, as Harris relates, was often noting in his diary how cross he was with himself for getting up late. He planned self-improvement, and strove hard to deny that the rational man could be influenced by the weather or season. It was left to his biographer, James Boswell, to observe that in fact Johnson was very weather-susceptible.

Samuel Johnson achieved a lot, even if he did get up later in the morning than he thought he should, so I offer this as comforting.

⌒⟋⟋◉

It's raining, it's pouring,
The old man's snoring . . .

⌒⟋⟋◉

It was just after the Winter Solstice when the two almost-elderly ladies, accompanied by three middle-aged cats, set off again westwards. Darren had warned of wind and flood but on the approach to Langport the floods were where they should have been, in the fields towards Muchelney, with only paddling-depth water across a stretch of road.

On arrival the cats did what they always do, that is, to shoot straight out into the garden. In summer their coming is bad for shrews, slow-worms or young birds, but by December hunting chances are diminished.

In the wood the snowdrops were in bud. The eldest of my cousin's sons, who has a nose for all things related to property, came over to look at the Disputed Territories. His advice was not to give an inch. He came up with an expression I had not heard before, 'development creep', and suggested further recourse to the Land Registry. Then came the best bit to my ears, that he would help deal with it.

I wanted to give Will, the builder, some wine to thank him for being so helpful with trying to keep the cottage dry (which, standing on wet moorland, it never will be), so rang to find out where he was. He turned out to be up at the top of St Mary's Church, Taunton, fixing ties to test how much the tower moves when the bells are ringing. Not an ideal place to receive wine. So I set out to find the parcel box outside his house, and in so doing came close to the flooded fields on either side of the river at Muchelney.

Flood tourism sounds callous, but the truth is floods across fields are beautiful and exciting to see, especially as this time, so far as I knew, no one's house was under water. The swans and gulls were riding the wavelets of these wide, temporary lakes. The light was grey and damp but the white birds shone out in their subfusc world.

Late in the year it rained so much that people asked afterwards why the Levels had not flooded as badly as a few years ago. The answer appears to be that this time, it was the right sort of rain. Or rather, that in 2013-14 it was the wrong sort, as far as this landscape

Mist on the Hill

is concerned, in that it may not have been always heavy, but it was non-stop. From 18 December 2013 to early March 2014 there was only one dry day. As John Rowlands the engineer told me, 'it is this constant daily topping up of the rivers which was so damaging, rather than the one-off deluge that other parts of the country saw'.

As I looked out across what I knew were really fields rather than lakes on Christmas Eve, there was no question of *deep and crisp and even*, things were very, very wet. It is true, though, that we did have intermittent dry days. The statistics John later shared with me confirmed that, overall, 2013–14 was a good bit wetter.

I was up at midnight so can report that, yet again, the animals did not break into human speech, as they are supposed to do at midnight on Christmas Eve. I wish they would, although there is a world-weary version of that myth in which, when the animals do speak, it is only to bicker and spread bad news. But why think so ill of them . . . we well know which species is most likely to do that.

For some years, Darren and I have driven to Bath to join my brother's family on Christmas Day. We aim to get there for tea, stopping on the way in Wells to allow me to hurry into the Vicars' Chapel for a short, spoken service. Darren, a no-nonsense atheist, remains in the car, resting from the rigours of the Christmas wine trade.

The Cathedral is shut in the afternoon, at rest from its own earlier rigours, but down at the end of the cobbled Vicars' Close the chapel is open for a short, quiet service, led by a lone clergy-man or, more often, woman. I imagine there is an element of the short straw to that particular duty. About half a dozen people gather there, giving the impression that they know the ropes . . . they are, for instance, good at an odd, delayed rhythm of reading the responses, which sounds like communicating by satellite.

The chapel, built between 1424 and 1430, is plain, small and comfortable, a good place to think of the past members of my family who were proper believers, traces of whose influence I have never really tried to throw off. We pray for the usual improbable things, world peace, or that our leaders may be righteous, but then more immediate subjects may come up; the plight of the people in Syria or Yemen, or of the natural world.

In no time the service is over and we are out in the Vicars' Close, a perfect street with tall-chimneyed houses even older than the chapel, facing each other across front gardens. An archway leads from it into the Cathedral Close. On wet Christmas afternoons it is deserted but this year the low sunlight was rosy and people and dogs were about. Back at the car Darren opens an eye and enquires, 'So was it over when you got there?' He is a naturally good time-keeper.

After that we go up over Mendip, along, then down into Bath. From the medieval beauty of Wells into the eighteenth-century beauty of Bath, it is a good journey, with a cheerful destination.

∾

Back in Langport, the brightness of Christmas was then swept away, so the Boxing Day walk I was proposing had lost its appeal. In truth, it was only to me that it had ever had much appeal. Instead of walking I spread out bunches of greenery and twigs already gathered from the wood and put together decorations for my cousin's long dining table, at which I was due to sit in the evening.

My uncle, my cousin's father, made her oak table and rush-seated chairs years ago, in an Arts and Crafts style. He was a brother of my mother and aunt, a skilled, gentle and inventive man. He is there in my aunt's photograph album, sometimes in naval uniform with pipe in mouth, or astride etiolated-looking motorbikes, or in the sailing boat he made with his brothers.

The muddled chronology of the uncaptioned album is confusing, but it mainly records holidays at the family seaside shack before and during the First World War. Although several of the men appear in uniform, the only hint of a wider world is a telescope set up on the Sussex shingle; otherwise it is all boating, bathing, hair-washing in a bowl set up on sticks, a spot of fancy dress and constant, mainly youthful company.

I was told little of what became of the people crowding those photographs. From lively and sociable the few I knew seemed to have become the opposite, very quiet and withdrawn. But by then they had gone through the first half of the twentieth century. To my knowledge, my uncle made a boat, some beds, invented a demountable 'igloo' henhouse constructed of metal panels, and some place mats. There must have been plenty more, but the long oak table, still standing in the room for which he designed it, is probably his masterpiece.

With a basket of winter posies but in some trepidation, I set off into the dark wet night to go to the farm. The three hazards I knew about were a corner of a lane that is often very wet, the sometimes misty hairpin bends as the road rises up the wooded hill, and the barking dogs that love to chase any cars that pass their farm, near to my cousin's. Generations of them have been barking and chasing cars since at least the 1950s, so that counts as a friendly hazard. On the way all was smooth, no flooding, no mist, no dogs.

On the way back, after a heartwarming evening, things were a lot more watery than before. My cousin, who has been driving in all weathers in that hilly district for more than sixty years, expressed no concern about my departing into the wet and pitchy night, so I took courage from that. It had been raining all evening, which may account for the dogs staying at home. But the mist now lay thick along the top and was doing what I particularly dislike on the way down, dancing in and out of the beech trees and across the zigzag road in opaque, wraithlike swirls.

Along the lane at the bottom water was bursting from the higher bank and making a divided stream, one part riffling across in a swift oblique flow into the opposite ditch, the other hurrying down to join the flood that had not been there a few hours before. The headlights shone on its brown wind-ruffled surface.

There had been no traffic until that moment but then a car from the other direction turned the corner. The driver paused to let me through, which gave no time for dithering. Game as ever, the car took to the water and, accompanied by lapping sounds, we reached the other side. Only later did I wonder if it had been good manners on the part of the other driver to let me go first, or a wily way to find out how deep the water was.

Looking from the upstairs window next morning, I could see the light gleaming on the river, which means that the water is very high. My cousin rang, anxious to hear I had not come to grief as, she now told me, does happen on that corner. It was only after hearing from one of her sons how much water he and his wife had encountered on their way home that she had wished she had sent me another way.

With only a short time left before returning to London, during which I planned to clear space for poplar planting and gather more apple scions, it seemed a shame to put off the purely recreational walk I wanted to take to the wood. Darren declined the treat of accompanying me, even just as far as the river, saying he no longer owns wellingtons. The idea of driving around the West Country as much as he does without wellingtons in the car seems to me astonishing . . . but then it is part of the fun for members of different generations to astonish each other.

It was about 2 p.m. when the rain fizzled out. I went through the garden gate on to the moor, then up the embankment to the brimming straw-brown river. It was rushing by, carrying leaves and branches with it; luckily nothing else. The sun was trying to break through a pearly sky, starlings were gathering on the rails of the sewage works, maybe waiting for more of their fellows to join them before setting off together for one of their roosting places among the reeds. Assuming they still have more fellows . . . my cousin had said the night before that the starlings have disappeared from the farm. I forgot to ask about the rabbits.

The river path was muddy, but not muddy enough to get boots stuck, except by the gates where the cows had crowded in autumn. My plan was to turn away from the river, pass the anglers' lake, then go through the fields rather than along the road. But, from the gateway into the field I had thought to cross, it looked better for canoeing than walking. Sheets of water stood bright between bristly bands of sedge, expanding to cover the whole centre ground.

Going by the road took longer. A slight mistiness was already gathering in the wood by the time I got there. There were some rooks and tits about, and the beginnings of snowdrops. When I had taken photographs among the hazels at the same time last year, the pink-brown of their fallen leaves had taken the chill off the grey images. Now, looking up into the same space, the picture is changed, with the big tree sprawled across, partly hiding the rose madder of the decaying leaves.

Slipping past the hazels, I went to greet yet another fallen tree. Until it came down, this one had been a puzzle to me . . . its bark and leaves suggested apple, but though it very occasionally blossomed I never saw any fruit on it. Until it fell, bringing to eye level a wealth of tiny green apples. So, a crab apple . . . it must have been at the top of its row in the old planting of Sugg's Orchard. Now it was lying down I could see what had been

invisible before, that its first trunk was completely hollow. All the subsequent growth, a lot of it, had been perching on the top rim of the hollow, in what I now recognise as a characteristic, never-say-die, apple gesture.

You can now look through the top rim, which is a sculpture in itself. Grey-green ridges of healthy wood appear to swirl down, looking like sea-washed rock, towards the turmoil below. But until it fell they were actually swirling upwards, the life of the old tree fighting to keep going under its bark, never mind the rot in the middle. And it looks as though it means to keep on fighting still, with enough sap somehow getting through from the small amount of trunk attached to the root.

From not having paid this tree much attention, I am suddenly very keen to see it survive, at least long enough to be able to take grafts from it. But this was a fleeting visit, just to wish it well, to say, hang on . . . Because it was no good loitering. From the top of the track the view already looked a deep murky grey-blue and, unlike last year, I was walking back.

For a change, and because I imagined it might be easier than the way I had come, I took the footpath to the east of Coombe. This was a mistake. If every step involves schlurping, tugging and trying not to overbalance in mud, progress is slow. If you start your return after four o'clock a few days after the Winter Solstice, slow progress means there is still a lot of mud between you and home when it is no longer possible to see very well.

Having struggled through what is normally my favourite part of that walk, between trees along a wide path, I thought that the greater openness of the rest of the way would make the going better. Not so, but it was too late to try to go back to the road. To be a pedestrian on that road at night is riskier than flailing through mud.

The path is full of character, looping along beside ditches, with a sluice gate serving as a bridge here, a stone stile there, a wooden walkway, frequent changes of direction and level. Many of these things are part of an outdated system of drainage which still contributes, in a modest way, to the more efficient arrangements engineered in the 1960s and 70s.

Being very keen on staying upright I sometimes had to hold on for balance, grasping through the gloom a bramble, a stone post, or some knotty emplacement of iron. Marvellously, there was always just enough light to see, even when very black clouds started assembling. By then the outline of the railway bridge over the river was looming up, beckoning with the promise that there was not much further to go.

There was one more cause for alarm as I squelched under the railway bridge and looked along the river. The reflected lights seemed in the wrong place, as though the water had flowed across the path. Trying to dismiss the idea of being cut off by new flooding, I trudged on. Getting nearer, it became easier to see that what I had assumed was a straight section of bank does in fact curve. The water being up to the brim meant there was more width within this curve for the lights to twinkle in.

How gratefully did I turn down from the embankment, open the garden gate and walk back up the narrow path towards the light spilling out from the kitchen.

Darren looked at me in disbelief when I related why I was so late, exclaiming, 'and you thought I would want to come with you in all that?'

Well no, I had not thought he would, knowing that a warm room and football on the telly was the alternative. There is no insisting that one's nearest and dearest will enjoy the wintry opalescent light on a full river, or the company of rooks, or getting home covered in mud to find the light on in the kitchen, the kettle to hand.

But a cup of tea, with some toast and marmite, that we could agree upon.

Afterword

IN MARCH 2020, WHEN COVID-19 WAS getting into its stride in Britain, I became doubtful about writing anything based in 2019. Noah, as far as we know, did not record his interests Before the Flood; he got on with preparing for and surviving it. But survival of COVID-19 meant staying at home; the perfect chance, as was relentlessly said, to *forge ahead* with a project. More in the spirit of carrying on than of forging, I did decide to keep going.

Then, magical things started happening; wild goats were coming into town, antlered deer sat at their ease in suburban front gardens, birdsong sounded louder, the air smelt better, the colours of spring were exceptionally bright, sea creatures could hear each other in the quieter oceans, the skies were almost free of traffic . . . Nature was right there, ready to make the most of a world temporarily less dominated by humans.

The wish to discover more about how nature is, or is not, surviving in a small piece of Somerset underpins this book.

Afterword

So these national and international instances of the natural world's readiness to bound back were cheering, especially as it was not my front garden the goats or deer had chosen. But the withdrawal of humankind could only be temporary. Knowing this reinforced the urgency of writing in favour of a more tolerant, less destructive attitude towards the multitude of other living beings on our planet.

Of the interrelated causes explaining the thinning and disappearance of species, I had thought that climate change would be the main one. As, underlyingly, it doubtless is. Looking outwards from the wood now, however, it appears that the more immediate causes of loss are the destruction of natural habitats, the effects of intensive agriculture, and of the international trade in live plants and animals.

None of these has to keep blundering on as they have been. Indeed, they had better not if there is to be much diversity of species left by 2050, when, or so we care to hope, a brake may have been put on global warming. It is not inevitable that we destroy the life around us, including ourselves. The first lockdown to try to prevent the spread of a virus (its progress aided by travel and trade) was an illustration of that.

Realists are good at pointing out that a global problem needs tackling on a global scale. Sometimes the other side of this coin is that individual efforts are futile, beyond making those individuals feel better. While I agree with the international scale, I disagree about the futility of small efforts, or the implied silliness of doing things to make ourselves feel better . . . feeling better has, after all, something to be said for it.

So I shall end with an example of a small effort that might do a scintilla of good. Insects are low down in the natural food chain, meaning that they are vital to it. Almost anyone can try to help them by letting a patch of grass, flowers or weeds grow tall and go to seed. There is no need to have four acres; pots on a windowsill or doorstep will do. On their own these patches remain patches, but the more there are, the more they could join up to help the flow of life to continue, across the deserts of concrete, of greed, and of uncertainty.

London, 2021

Acknowledgements

Thank You Very Much to all the many people who have helped with the research and writing of this book, including those who did not know they were helping. They range from the child who, just as I was trying to remember seasonal rhymes, passed the front garden singing *It's raining, it's pouring,* to all those I consulted, either in person or print. I am a grateful magpie. And, I hope, a fairly accurate one, but any errors are sure to be mine.

In particular I would like to thank Sue Gee for her constant encouragement, Sophie Scard of United Agents and Matt Casbourne of Duckworth (with all the Duckworth team) for believing in the book and working on it so judiciously. And Alison Britton for kindly vigilance and company from across the street (never more important than of late).

In person I have had invaluable help from Robert Dunning, Roger Dickey, Catherine Mowat, John Bebbington, Ron Scamp, Julia Davies, Rob Walrond, Pat Twiney, Shirley Nicholas, Linda Elphick, Tony Anderson, David Crossman, Graham Lock, James Cross, Fleming Ulf-Hansen, Caroline Dunn, Jeremy Harvey, while through written communications, Helen Bostock, John Rowlands, Diana Bell, Samantha Norris, Gabriel Hemery, Julian Orbach, Stephen Maddalena, David Sutcliffe and Rob Wilson-North have all been very helpful. I would also like to include those from whose books or radio programmes I have quoted.

The wood is nothing if not a practical project, so the work of Steve Joyce, Les Davies and Laura Small are of the essence, as is the nearby presence of Doreen, Philip and Suzanne Knight, Guy Smith and Laura Evans of Higher Plot Vineyard, John and Jenny Whitfield, and the support of Will Saunders, the builder and Dave Locke, the mower expert . . . thank you.

Which leaves the equally essential element of family and friends. In the unnerving time of COVID-19 it has been the knowledge that you are still there that has kept me going (apart from the company of cats and the BBC). So, thank you all, especially Martin and Louise Pavey, my cousin Heather Stallard and her family and my nephews and their families. I hope there is no one I have left out. Lastly, my thanks go to my dear son Darren, whose name and some aspects of whose character I have taken the liberty of including in this book, despite the risk of his disapproval.

Appendix A: Plants

Visit by Catherine Mowat on 21/4/19 to provide species list for land on Aller Hill.

Trees which have clearly been planted have not been included.

Abundance of plants on site: R=rare, O=occasional, F=frequent, LF=locally frequent, D=dominant

WOODED AREAS		
Scientific name	Abundance	Common name
Acer campestre	R	Field maple
Arctium minus	R	Lesser burdock
Arum maculatum	O	Lords and Ladies
Asplenium scolopendrium	O	Hart's-tongue fern
Brachypodium sylvaticum	O	False wood brome
Circaea lutetiana	O	Enchanter's nightshade
Clematis vitalba	O	Traveller's joy
Cornus sanguinea	R	Dogwood
Corylus avellana	O, LD	Hazel
Crataegus monogyna	R	Hawthorn
Daphne laureola	R	Spurge laurel
Ficaria verna	R	Lesser celandine
Fraxinus excelsior	F	Ash
Galium aparine	F	Cleavers
Geum urbanum	R	Herb bennet
Glechoma hederacea	R	Ground ivy

Hedera helix	F	Ivy
Iris foetidissima	O	Stinking iris
Ligustrum vulgare	O	Wild privet
Mentha sp. (introduced)	R	Mint
Narcissus sp. (introduced)	R	Daffodil
Polystichum setiferum	R	Soft shield fern
Prunus species	R	Wild plum/apple?
Prunus spinosa	O	Blackthorn
Rubus fruticosus agg.	LD	Blackberry
Rumex sanguineus	F	Wood dock
Sambucus nigra	F	Elder
Sherardia arvensis	R	Madder
Tamus communis	O	Black bryony
Urtica dioica	O, LF	Common nettle
Veronica chamaedrys	R	Germander speedwell
Viburnum lantana	R	Wayfaring tree

Canopy dominated by ash, locally hazel is dominant. Occasional seedlings to 30cm tall, no saplings or young canopy trees.

GRASSY AREAS		
Scientific name	Abundance	Common name
Agrimonia eupatoria	R	Agrimony
Agrostis capillaris	O	Common bent
Agrostis stolonifera	F	Creeping bent
Anacamptis pyramidalis	R	Pyramical orchid *reported by Ruth
Anthoxanthum odoratum	O	Sweet vernal-grass

Appendix A: Plants

Arum maculatum	O	Lords and ladies
Bellis perennis	R	Daisy
Brachypodium sylvaticum	F	False wood-brome
Carex flacca	R	Glaucous sedge*
Cerastium fontanum	R	Common mouse-ear
Cirsium arvense	LF	Creeping thistle
Cirsium vulgare	R	Spear thistle
Clematis vitalba	LF	Traveller's joy
Cynosurus cristatus	O	Crested dog's-tail
Dactylis glomerata	F	Cock's-foot
Festuca rubra	R	Red fescue
Galium aparine	LF	Cleavers
Geranium dissectum	O	Cut-leaved cranesbill
Geranium robertianum	R	Herb-robert
Geum urbanum	O	Herb bennet
Glechoma hederacea	O	Ground ivy
Hedera helix	O	Ivy
Helminthothica echioides	R	Bristly ox-tongue
Heracleum sphondylium	R	Hogweed
Holcus lanatus	F	Yorkshire fog
Hyacinthoides hispanica	R	Spanish bluebell
Iris foetidissima	O	Stinking iris
Lathyrus pratensis	R	Meadow vetchling*
Lolium perenne	O	Perennial rye-grass
Muscari armeniacum	R	Grape-hyacinth
Myosotis sylvatica	R	Wood forget-me-not
Narcissus sp.	R	Daffodil

Plantago lanceolata	R	Ribwort plantain
Plantago major	R	Broadleaf plantain
Plantago media	R	Hoary plantain*
Poa annua	O	Annual meadow-grass
Potentilla reptans	O	Creeping cinqfoil
Prunella vulgaris	O	Self-heal
Prunus spinosa seedling	O	Blackthorn
Ranunculus acris	O	Meadow buttercup
Ranunculus repens	F	Creeping buttercup
Rumex crispus	LF	Curled dock
Rumex sanguineus	LF	Wood dock
Sonchus sp.	R	Sow-thistle species
Taraxacum agg.	O	Dandelion
Trifolium repens	O	White clover
Urtica dioica	LF	Common nettle
Veronica serpyllifolia	R	Thyme-leaved speedwell
Vicia sativa	R	Common vetch
Viola odorata	R	Sweet violet
Viola riviana	R	Early dog violet

* denotes species indicative of unimproved calcareous to neutral grassland (on rock outcrop)

POND, POND BANKS AND DAMP AREAS		
Scientific name	Abundance	Common name
Anthriscus sylvestris	R	Cow-parsley
Asplenium scolopendrium	O	Hart's-tongue fern
Berula erecta	F	Lesser water-parsnip

Caltha palustris	R	Kingcup
Calystegia sepium	O	Hedge bindweed
Cardamine flexuosa	R	Wavy bittercress
Carex pendula	O	Pendulous sedge
Chara sp.	O	Stonewort species
Dryopteris dilatata	R	Broad buckler-fern
Dryopteris filix-mas	R	Common male-fern
Epilobium hirsutum	O	Great willowherb
Epilobium sp.	O	Willowherb species
Eupatorium cannabinum	O	Hemp agrimony
Filipendula ulmaria	R	Meadowsweet
Galium aparine	F	Cleavers
Iris pseudacorus	R	Flag iris
Juncus effusus	R	Soft rush
Juncus inflexus	O	Hard rush
Juncus subnodulosus	R	Blunt-flowered rush
Leucanthemum vulgare	R	Ox-eye daisy
Mentha aquatica	R	Water mint
Persicaria hydropiper	R	Water-pepper
Phragmites australis	R	Common reed
Primula vulgaris x veris	R	False oxlip
Salix cinerea	R	Grey willow
Scrophularia auriculata	O	Water figwort
Silene dioica	R	Red campion
Solanum dulcemara	R	Bittersweet
Sparganium erectum	O	Branched bur-reed
Urtica dioica	F	Common nettle

Some of the plants planted around the caravan (introduced and native)
Galanthus sp. – Snowdrop variety
Vinca sp. – Periwinkle
Helleborus sp. – hellebore species
Hyacinthoides non-scripta – bluebell
Hyacinthoides non-scripta x hispanica – Spanish bluebell
Dipsacus fullonum – teasel
Symphytum sp. – comfrey species

Appendix B: Birds

ORNITHOLOGICAL SURVEY (BREEDING BIRD SURVEY)

Date: 22 May 2019	Surveyor(s): Roger Dickey	Survey Number: N/A	Weather:	
Time: Start: 09:00 Finish: 11:00			**Overnight:** Clear, cold **Moon:** Waning Gibbous	**Survey:** **Cloud:** Nil **Wind:** Light **Rain:** Nil **Temperature:** 11°c

Evidence of Predator/Predation: Nil

Man-made Disturbance: Nil

Species	Count	Territories (Est)	Evidence of Breeding	Notes
Jackdaw	8	3	Early juveniles	Orchard and wood
Magpie	2	1		Top of wood
Rook	25		Mostly fledged juveniles	From above the wood
Goldfinch	4	2	Carrying food	
Chiffchaff	6	3	Carrying food	No song
Pheasant	1			

Great Tit	7	5	Using nest holes and carry-ing food	
Blue Tit	3	3 min	2 x juv, adult w/ food	
Wren	6	4	Males singing	
Stock Dove	4	2		Males calling simultaneously
Blackbird	6	4	Adults with food to nest	
Starling	1		Juv	Roosting
Woodpigeon	4			Roosting
Buzzard	1			Nest off site. Hunting
Blackcap	3	3	Singing males	
Jay	2	1 or 2		Separate birds calling
Long-tailed Tits	12	2	Juveniles in majority	Two flocks seen.
Robin	5	5	Males singing	
Chaffinch	2	1	Adults carry-ing food	

Appendix B: Birds

Treecreeper	3	3		Single adults in different areas
Spotted Flycatcher	1	?		Single bird feeding on edge of wood.
Control: **Nil**				

Corpse Control: D – Decomposing, I – Injured, P – Predated,
E – Entire, Fxx – number of feathers.

Appendix C: Moths

Common name	Scientific name	Quantity
Diamond-back Moth	Plutella xylostella	1
Common Plume	Emmelina monodactyla	1
Chequered Fruit-tree Tortrix	Pandemis corylana	1
(No common name)	Agapeta hamana	1
(No common name)	Euzophera pinguis	1
Mother of Pearl	Pleuroptya ruralis	1
(No common name)	Chrysoteuchia culmella	7
(No common name)	Agriphila tristella	1
Dwarf Cream Wave	Idaea fuscovenosa	2
Small Fan-footed Wave	Idaea biselata	1
Dark-barred Twin-spot Carpet	Xanthorhoe ferrugata	2
Yellow Shell	Camptogramma bilineata	1
Small Waved Umber	Horisme vitalbata	1
Pretty Chalk Carpet	Melanthia procellata	1
Brimstone Moth	Opisthograptis luteolata	2
Dusky Thorn	Ennomos fuscantaria	2
Willow Beauty	Peribatodes rhomboidaria	3
Straw Dot	Rivula sericealis	2
Rosy Footman	Miltochrista miniata	4

Appendix C: Moths

Dingy Footman	Eilema griseola	4
Svensson's Copper Underwing	Amphipyra berbera	1
Mouse Moth	Amphipyra tragopoginis	1
Dark Arches	Apamea monogly-pha	1
Common Wainscot	Mythimna pallens	1
Flame Shoulder	Ochropleura plecta	2
Large Yellow Underwing	Noctua pronuba	1
Lesser Broad-bordered Yellow Underwing	Noctua janthe	12
Setaceous Hebrew Character	Xestia c-nigrum	3
Uncertain/Rustic agg.	Hoplodrina alsines/blanda	1
Common Rustic agg.	Mesapamea secalis agg.	4
	Species:	30
	Numbers:	66

ALSO

Rufous Grasshopper	Gomphocerippus rufus	1
Dung Beetle	Geotrupes stercorarius	1

Bibliography

Bartram, W., *Travels of William Bartram*, 1791,
Dover Publications Inc., 1955.

Benson, P., *The Levels*, Constable, 1987.

Burns, H., Holden, P. and Sharrock J.T.R., *The RSPB
Handbook of British Birds*, Pan Macmillan, 1982.

Chetwode, P., *Two Middle-Aged Ladies in Andalusia*,
John Murray, 1963.

Chinery, M. and Hargreaves, B., *Butterflies & Moths*, Collins
Gem Guides, 1981.

Cocker, M., *Our Place*, Vintage, 2018.

Conrad Gothie, S., *Damsons*, Prospect Books, 2018.

Coombes, A., and Hillier, J., *Hillier Manual of Trees
and Shrubs*, David & Charles, 1972.

Davies, P. and Gibbons, B., *Field Guide to Wild Flowers*,
Crowood Press, 1994.

Davies, N., *Cuckoo*, Bloomsbury, 2015.

Ekwall, E., *The Concise Oxford Dictionary of English Place-names*,
Oxford, 1936.

Gwatkin, E.N. and Johns, Rev. C. A., *Flowers in the Field*,
Routledge, 1907.

Hahnewald, E. and Hutchinson, J., *Wild Flowers in Colour*,
Penguin, 1958.

Harris, A., *Weatherland*, Thames & Hudson, 2015.

Bibliography

Hemery, G. and Simblet, S., *The New Sylva*, Bloomsbury, 2014.

Juniper, B. and Mabberley, D.J., *The Story of the Apple*, Timber Press, 2006.

Kasabova, K., *Border*, Granta, 2017.

Kingsbury, N., *Daffodil*, Timber Press, 2013.

Laidler, K., *Squirrels in Britain*, David & Charles, 1980.

Leach, P., *Roman Somerset*, The Dovecote Press, 2001.

McCarthy, M., *The Moth Snowstorm*, John Murray, 2015.

Merryweather, R., *The Bramley*, private publication, 1992.

Monbiot, G., *Feral*, Allen Lane, 2013.

Newton, I., *Farming and Birds*, Collins New Naturalist Library, 2017.

Rackham, O., *The Illustrated History of the Countryside*, Weidenfeld & Nicolson, 1994.

Rebanks, J., *English Pastoral*, Allen Lane, 2020.

Sackville-West, V., *V. Sackville-West's Garden Book*, Michael Joseph, 1968.

Sebald, W.G., *Austerlitz*, Penguin, 2002.

Skea, R., *Monet's Trees*, Thames & Hudson, 2015.

Skelmersdale, C., *A Gardeners' Guide to Bulbs*, The Crowood Press, 2012.

Tree, I., *Wilding*, Picador, 2018.

Trollope, A., *The Warden*, Longman, 1855.

Twiney, P., *As I Remember...* private publication, 2014.

Watkins, A., *The Old Straight Track*, Methuen, 1925.

West, K., *Saving the Season*, Knopf, 2013.

Wohlleben, P., *The Hidden Life of Trees*, Greystoke Books, 2016.

Websites consulted include:
British Geological Survey, www.bgs.ac.uk
BBC Radio 4, Costing the Earth, Run Rabbit,
www.bbc.co.uk/programmes/b0b2jg2r (16/05/2018)
Butterfly Conservation, www.butterfly-conservation.org
Forestry Commission, www.forestresearch.gov.uk
Lovell Stone Group, www.lovellstonegroup.com
The Mammal Society, www.mammal.org.uk
Plantlife, www.plantlife.org.uk
Royal Horticultural Society, www.rhs.org.uk/plantsforbugs
Royal Society for the Protection of Birds, www.rspb.org.uk
Woodland Trust, www.woodlandtrust.org.uk

to Bridgwater

Aller
Drove

Aller

The Seed
× Factory

Bow

Aller
Escarpment

✝ Aller Church

Aller Moor

where the
cranes feed

River Parrett

Angle
Lake

Penzance ← Railway → Lond

Rough Map
of the area, including
ALLER, LANGPORT
and LOW HAM,
Somerset

Curry Rivel Escarpment

Burton Pynsent
Monument

← Taunton

Curry Rivel